BEFORE THE WAR

LECTOR HOUSE PUBLIC DOMAIN WORKS

This book is a result of an effort made by Lector House towards making a contribution to the preservation and repair of original classic literature. The original text is in the public domain in the United States of America, and possibly other countries depending upon their specific copyright laws.

In an attempt to preserve, improve and recreate the original content, certain conventional norms with regard to typographical mistakes, hyphenations, punctuations and/or other related subject matters, have been corrected upon our consideration. However, few such imperfections might not have been rectified as they were inherited and preserved from the original content to maintain the authenticity and construct, relevant to the work. The work might contain a few prior copyright references as well as page references which have been retained, wherever considered relevant to the part of the construct. We believe that this work holds historical, cultural and/or intellectual importance in the literary works community, therefore despite the oddities, we accounted the work for print as a part of our continuing effort towards preservation of literary work and our contribution towards the development of the society as a whole, driven by our beliefs.

We are grateful to our readers for putting their faith in us and accepting our imperfections with regard to preservation of the historical content. We shall strive hard to meet up to the expectations to improve further to provide an enriching reading experience.

Though, we conduct extensive research in ascertaining the status of copyright before redeveloping a version of the content, in rare cases, a classic work might be incorrectly marked as not-in-copyright. In such cases, if you are the copyright holder, then kindly contact us or write to us, and we shall get back to you with an immediate course of action.

HAPPY READING!

BEFORE THE WAR

RICHARD BURTON HALDANE (VISCOUNT HALDANE)

ISBN: 978-93-90314-10-2

Published: 1920

© 2020
LECTOR HOUSE LLP

LECTOR HOUSE LLP
E-MAIL: lectorpublishing@gmail.com

VISCOUNT HALDANE

SECRETARY OF STATE FOR WAR FROM DECEMBER, 1905 TO
JUNE, 1912;
LORD HIGH CHANCELLOR FROM JUNE, 1912 TO MAY, 1915.

BEFORE THE WAR

BY

VISCOUNT HALDANE

PREFATORY NOTE

The chapters of which this little volume consists were constructed with a definite purpose. It was to render clear the line of thought and action followed by the Government of this country before the war, between January, 1906, and August, 1914. The endeavor made was directed in the first place to averting war, and in the second place to preparing for it as well as was practicable if it should come. In reviewing what happened I have made use of the substance of various papers recently contributed to the *Westminster Gazette*, the *Atlantic Monthly*, *Land and Water*, and the *Sunday Times*. The gist of these, which were written with their inclusion in this book in view, has been incorporated in the text together with other material. I have to thank the Editors of these journals for their courtesy in agreeing that the substance of what they published should be made use of here as part of a connected whole.

CONTENTS

LIST OF ILLUSTRATIONS

CHAPTER I

INTRODUCTION

The purpose of the pages which follow is, as I have said in the Prefatory Note, to explain the policy pursued toward Germany by Great Britain through the eight years which immediately preceded the great war of 1914. It was a policy which had two branches, as inseparable as they were distinct. The preservation of peace, by removing difficulties and getting rid of misinterpretations, was the object of the first branch. The second branch was concerned with what might happen if we failed in our effort to avert war. Against any outbreak by which such failure might be followed we had to insure. The form of the insurance had to be one which, in our circumstances, was practicable, and care had to be taken that it was not of a character that would frustrate the main purpose by provoking, and possibly accelerating, the very calamity against which it was designed to provide.

The situation was delicate and difficult. The public most properly expected of British Ministers that they should spare no effort for peace and for security. It was too sensible to ask for every detail of the steps taken for the attainment of this end. There are matters on which it is mischievous to encourage discussion, even in Parliament. Members of Parliament know this well, and are sensible about it. The wisest among them do not press for open statements which if made to the world would imperil the very object which Parliament and the public have directed those responsible to them to seek to attain. What is objected to in secret diplomacy hardly includes that which from its very nature must be negotiated in the first instance between individuals.

The policy actually followed was in principle satisfactory to the great majority of our people. To them it was familiar in its general outlines. But for the minority, which included both our pacifists and our chauvinists, it was either too much or too little. For, on the one hand, its foundation was the theory that, amid the circumstances of Europe in which it had to be built up, human nature could not be safely relied on unswervingly to resist warlike impulses. On the other hand, this peril notwithstanding, it was the considered view of those responsible that war neither ought to be regarded as being inevitable, nor was so in fact. It was quite true that the development of military preparations had been so great as to make Europe resemble an armed camp; but, if actual conflict could be averted, the burden this state of things implied ought finally to render its continuance no longer tolerable. What was really required was that unbroken peace should be preserved, and the hand of time left to operate.

In the course of history it has rarely been the case that any war that has broken out was really inevitable, and there does not appear to be any sufficient reason for thinking that the war of 1914 was an exception to the general rule. It seems clear that, if Germany had resolved to do so, she could quite safely have abstained from entering upon it and from encouraging Austria in a mad adventure. The reason why the war came appears to have been that at some period in the year 1913 the German Government finally laid the reins on the necks of men whom up to then it had held in restraint. The decision appears to have been allowed at this point to pass from civilians to soldiers. I do not believe that even then the German Government as a whole intended deliberately to invoke the frightful consequences of actual war, even if it seemed likely to be victorious. But I do believe that it elected to take the risk of what it thought improbable, a general resistance by the Entente Powers if Germany were to threaten to use her great strength. In thus departing in 1913 from the appearance of self-restraint which in the main they had displayed up to then, the Emperor and his Ministers misjudged the situation. They did not foresee the crisis to which their policy was conducting, and when that crisis arrived they lost their heads and blundered in trying to deal with it. They did not perceive the whirlpool toward which they were heading. They thought that they could safely expose what was precarious to a strain, and secure the substance of a real victory without having to overcome actual resistance. Had they put an extreme ambition for their country aside, and been careful in their language to others, they might have attained a considerable success without a shot being fired. But they were over ambitious and in their language they were far from careful. A few unlucky words made all the difference in the concluding days of July, 1914:

"Ten lines, a statesman's life in each."

We here had done the best we could, according to our lights, to keep Germany from misjudging us. It was not always easy to do this. The genius of our people was not well adapted for the particular task. If the only question to-day were whether we always rendered ourselves intelligible to her, she might say with some show of reason that we did not. She might have grumbled, as Bismarck used to do, over our apparent indefiniteness. But that indefiniteness in policy was only apparent. Its form was due to the habit of mind which was, what it always has been and probably always will be, the habit of mind of the people of these islands. It was the defect of her qualities that prevented Germany from understanding what this habit of mind truly imported, and we have never fully taken in at any period of our history how little she has ever understood it. Let anyone who doubts this read the German memoirs which have appeared since the war. But it remains not the less true and obvious that the purpose of the British Government which fashioned the policy in question was to leave no stone unturned in the endeavor to find a way of keeping the peace between Germany and the Entente Powers. Now success in that endeavor was not a certainty, and it was necessary to insure against the risk of failure. The second branch of British policy related to the provision for defense rendered imperative by the element of uncertainty which was unavoidable. The duty of the Government of this country was to make sure that, if their endeavor to preserve peace failed, the country should be prepared, in the best way of those that were practicable, to face the situation that might emerge.

Impetuous persons ask why, if there was even a chance of a great European war in which we might be involved, we did not appreciate the magnitude of what was at stake, and, laying everything else aside, concentrate our efforts on the immediate fashioning of such vast military forces as we possessed toward the end of the war? The answer will be found in the fourth chapter. We were aware of the risk, and we took what we thought the best means to meet it. Had we tried to do what we are reproached for not having done, we must have become weaker before we could have become stronger. For this statement I have given the military reasons. In a time of peace, even if the country had assented to the attempt being made, it is certain that we could not have accomplished such a purpose without long delay. It is probable that the result would have been failure, and it is almost certain that we should have provoked a "preventive war" on the part of Germany, a war not only with a very fair prospect, as things then stood, of a German success, but with something else that would have looked like the justification of a German effort to prevent that country from being encircled. Such a war would, with equal likelihood, have been the outcome even of the proclamation at such a time of a military alliance between the Entente Powers.

Other critics, belonging to a wholly different school of political thought, ask why we moved at all, and why we did not adhere to the good old policy of holding aloof from interference in Continental affairs. The answer is simple. The days when "splendid isolation" was possible were gone. Our sea power, even as an instrument of self-defense, was in danger of becoming inadequate in the absence of friendships which should insure that other navies would remain neutral if they did not actively co-operate with ours. It was only through the medium of such friendships that ultimate naval preponderance could be secured. The consciousness of that fact pervaded the Entente. With those responsible for the conduct of tremendous affairs probability has to be the guide of life. The question is always not what ought to happen but what is most likely to happen.

On the details of the diplomatic aspect of our endeavor, and on the spirit in which it was sought to carry it out, the second and third chapters of the book may serve to throw some light. The fourth chapter relates to the strategical plan, worked out after much consideration, for the possible event of failure. The plan was throughout based on the maintenance of superior sea power as the paramount instrument. As is indicated, the conservation of sufficient sea power implied as essential close and friendly relations with France, and also with Russia. Had there been no initial reason for the Entente policy, to be found in the desire to get rid of all causes of friction with these two great nations, the preservation of the prospect of continuing able to command the sea in war would in itself have necessitated the Entente. This conclusion was the result of the stocktaking of their assets for self-defense which the Entente Powers had to make when confronted with the growing organization for war of the Central Powers.

To set up the balancing of Powers as a principle was what we in this country would have been glad to have avoided had it been practicable to do so. We should have preferred the freedom of our old position of "splendid isolation." But the growing preparations of the Central Powers compelled Great Britain, France, and Russia to think of safety for each of them severally as to be secured only by treating such safety as a common interest. In the face of a new and growing danger we dared not leave ourselves to the risk of being dealt with in detail. The first thing to be done was, if possible, to convince the Central Powers that it would be to their own advantage to come to a complete agreement with us, an agreement of a business character, analogous to that which Lord Lansdowne had so satisfactorily concluded with France, and accompanied by cessation of the reasons which had led them to pile up armaments. There were highly influential persons in Germany who were far from averse to the suggested business arrangement. The armament question presented greater difficulty in that country, largely because of its tradition. But its solution was vital, for there were also those in Germany whose aim was to dispute with Great Britain the possession of the trident. Now for us, who constituted the island center of a scattered Empire, and who depended for food and raw materials on freedom to sail our ships, the question of sea power adequate for security was one of life or death. We could not sit still and allow Germany so to increase her navy in comparison with ours that she could make other Powers believe that their safest course was to throw in their lot and join their fleets with hers. We were bound to seek to make and maintain friendships, and to this end not only to preserve our margin of strength at sea, but to make ourselves able, if it became essential, to help our friends in case of aggression, thereby securing ourselves. That was the new situation which in the final result the old military spirit in Germany had created.

The balance of power is a dangerous principle; a general friendship between all Great Powers, or, better still, a League of the Nations, is by far preferable. But that consideration does not touch the actual point, which is that we did not seek to set up the principle of balancing that has given rise to so many questions. It was forced on us and was a sheer necessity of the situation. We did all we could to avoid it by negotiations with Germany, which, had they succeeded in the end, would have relieved France and Russia as much as ourselves and would have prevented the war.

Our efforts to preserve the peace ended in failure. The cause of that failure was nothing that we failed to do or that France did. It was proximately Austrian recklessness and indirectly, but just as strongly, German ambition. A real desire in July, 1914, on the part of the Central Powers to avoid war would have averted it. That Serbia may have been a provocative neighbor is no answer to the reproaches made to-day against the old Governments in Vienna and Berlin. They failed to take the steps requisite if peace were to be preserved.

People ask why the British Government between 1906 and 1914 did not discuss in public a situation which it understood well, and appeal to the nation. The answer is that to have done so would have been greatly to increase the difficulty of averting war. Up to the middle of 1913 the indications were that it was far from unlikely that war might in the result be averted. That was the view of some, both here and on the Continent, who were most competent to judge, men who had real opportunities for close observation from day to day. It is a view which is not in material conflict with anything we have since learned. The question whether war is inevitable has always been, as Bismarck more than once insisted, one for the statesmen of the countries concerned, and not for the soldiers and sailors who have a restricted field to work in, and for whom it is in consequence difficult to see things as a whole. Nor does great importance attach to-day to the triumphant declarations of those who, having chanced to guess aright, take pride in the cheap title to wisdom which has become theirs after the event. Still less does respect attach to the small but noisy minority in each of the countries concerned who in the years before 1914 were continuously contributing to bringing war on our heads by expressions of dislike to neighboring nations, and by prophecies that war with them must come. In the main Germany was worse in this feature than ourselves. But there were those here whose language made them useful propagandists for the German military party, to whom they were of much service.

Few wars are really inevitable. If we knew better how we should be careful to comport ourselves it may be that none are so. But extremists, whether chauvinist or pacifist, are not helpful in avoiding wars. That is because human nature is what it is.

Those who had to make the effort to keep the peace failed. But that neither shows that they ought not to have tried with all the strength they possessed in the way they did, nor that they would have done better had they discussed delicate details in public. There are topics and conjunctures in the almost daily changing relations between Governments as to which silence is golden. For however proper it may be in point of broad principle that the people should be fully informed of what concerns them vitally, the most important thing is those to whom they have confided their concerns should be given the best chance of success in averting danger to their interests. To have said more in Parliament and on the platform in the years in question, or to have said it otherwise, would have been to run grave risks of more than one sort. It is my strong impression that Lord Grey of Fallodon took the only course that was practicable, and that, had the danger of the catastrophe to be faced again and for the first time, the course he took would, even in the light of all we know to-day, again afford the best chance of avoiding it. He succeeded in improving greatly for the time the relations between this country and Germany, and but for the outbreak in the Near East he would probably have succeeded in navigating the dangerous waters successfully. The chance was far from being a hopeless one, and subsequent study of the facts has strengthened my impression that down to at least about the middle of the year 1913 the chances were substantially in his favor. A sufficiency at least of the leaders in other countries were co-operating with him, not all the leaders, but those who were in reality most important. The war when it came was due, not only to the failure of certain of the prominent men in the capitals of the Central Powers to adhere to principles to which for a long time they had held fast, but to the accident of untoward circumstances and the contingency that is inseparable from human affairs.

Such are some of the reasons which have led me to say what I have tried to express in the pages which follow. I have never been able to bring myself to believe that there are vast differences between the ways of thinking and habits of mind of the great and most highly civilized peoples of Europe. I have seen something of the Germans, and what I have learned of them and of their history has led me to the conclusion that, certain traditions of theirs notwithstanding, they resemble us more than they differ from us. If this be so, the sooner we take advantage of our present victory by seeking to turn our eyes from the past as far as can be, and to look steadily toward a future in which the misery and sin which that past saw shall be dwelt on to the least extent that is practicable, the better it will be for ourselves as well as for the rest of the world.

That world has been reminded of a great truth which had been partly forgotten by those whose faith lay in militarism. It is that to set up might as the foundation of right may in the end be to inspire those around with a passionate desire to hold such might in check and to overcome it. Democracy is not a system that lends itself easily to scientific preparation for war, but when democratic nations are really aroused their staying power, just because it rests on a true General Will, is without rival. The latent force in humanity which has its foundation in ethical idealism is the greatest of all forces for the vindication of right. German militarism managed to fail to understand this. Let us take pains to show our late enemies that if they make it clear that they have extinguished such militarism in a lasting fashion, the quarrel with them is at an end.

I am far from thinking that we here are perfect in our habits as a nation. We are apt not to keep in view how what we do is likely to look to others. We are somewhat deficient in the faculty of self-examination and self-criticism. Want of clarity of ground-principle in higher ideals is apt to prove a hindrance to more than the individual only. It generally brings with it want of clarity in the sense of social obligation. And this sometimes extends even to our relations to other countries.

It leads to our being misinterpreted as a nation. We have suffered a good deal in the past from having attributed to us motives which were not ours. The reason was the assumption that the apparent absence of definiteness in national purpose must have been designed as a cover for hidden and selfish ends. It is not true. We are indeed very insular, and what has been called the international mind is not common among the people of these islands. But we are kindly at heart, and when we have seemed self-regarding it has been simply because we were not conscious of our own limitations and had not much appreciation of the modes of thought of other people. We have paid the penalty for this defect at periods in our history. At one time France suspected us, I think in the main unjustly. Later on Germany suspected us, I think of a certainty unjustly. Now these things arise in part at least from our reputation for a particular kind of disposition, our supposed habitual and deliberately adopted desire to wait until the particular international situation of the moment should show how we could profit, before we gave any assurance as to the way in which we should act. What has given rise to this misunderstanding of our attitude in our relations to other countries is simply an exemplification of what has prevented us from fully understanding ourselves. It is our gift to be able to apply ourselves in emergencies, at home and abroad, with immense energy, and our success in promptly pulling ourselves together and coping with the unexpected has often suggested to outsiders that we had long ago looked ahead.

This has been said of us on the Continent. It is not so. We do not study the art of fishing in troubled waters. The waiting habit in our transactions, domestic as well as foreign, arises from our inveterate preference for thinking in images rather than in concepts. We put off decisions until the whole of the facts can be visualized. This carries with it that we often do not act until it is very late. Our gifts enable us to move with energy, if not always with precision. To predict what we will do in a given case is not easy for a foreigner. It is not easy even for ourselves. We have few abstract principles, and reliable induction from our past is not easy. We are often guided by what Mr. Justice Wendell Holmes has called "the intuition more subtle than any particular major premise." Nor is help to be derived from any study of our general outlook on life, for that outlook is hard to formulate even to ourselves.

Now all this, our peculiar gift, if kept under control, may well have its practical advantage, but, as the case stands, it is apt to bring in its train a good deal of disadvantage. In periods when nations are trying to render firm the basis of peace by remolding and giving precision to their aims, so that these can be made common aims, lack of definiteness in national ideals is a sure source of embarrassment. At a time when democracy is more and more claiming in terms to occupy the whole field it becomes increasingly desirable that the higher purposes of democracy should become clear to the people themselves. For the practise of a country can never be wholly divorced from its theory of life. The tendencies of the national will are bound up with the nation's science, with its literature, with its art, and with its religion. These tendencies are affected by the capacity of the nation to understand and express its own soul. Beyond science, literature, art and religion there lies something that may be called the national philosophy, a disposition rather than a definite creed. This sort of philosophy is different in France from what it is in Germany, and in Germany from what it is in the English-speaking countries. The philosophy of a people takes shape in the attitude its leaders adopt in their estimation of values and of the order in which they should be placed. And this turns on the conceptions and ideas which are current in the various departments of mental activity. It is thus that a philosophy of life has to be given some sort of place in his professions even by the statesman who has to address Parliament and the public. He is driven to make speeches in which a good many conceptions and ideas have to be brought together. And it gives rise to a great difference of quality in such utterances if the general outlook of the speaker be a large one. But this requires that he should know himself and be aware of the conceptions and ideas which dominate his mind, and should have examined their scope before employing them.

How some of those who were deeply responsible for the conduct of affairs tried to think in the anxious years before the war, and how they endeavored to apply their conclusions, is what I have endeavored to state in the course of what follows. They doubtless made mistakes and fell short of accomplishment in what they were aiming at. It is human so to do. But they tried what seemed to them the wisest course, and I have yet to learn that it was practicable to have followed any different course without a failure worse than any that occurred. After all, in the end the British Empire won, however hard it had to fight.

CHAPTER II
DIPLOMACY BEFORE THE WAR

If in this chapter I speak frequently in the first person and of my own part in the negotiations which it records, it is not from any desire to make prominent either my own personality or the part it fell to me to play. The reason is that I have endeavored to write of what I myself heard and saw, and that in consequence most of what follows is, for the sake of accuracy, largely transcribed from my personal diaries and records made at the time when the events to which they related took place. So frequent an employment of the personal pronoun as has been made in these pages would ordinarily be a blemish in taste, if not in style also, but in this case it seemed safer not to try to avoid it.

Many things that happened in the years just before 1914, as well as the events of the great war itself, are still too close to permit of our studying them in their full context. But before much time has passed the historians will have accumulated material that will overflow their libraries, and their hands will remain occupied for generations to come. At this moment all that safely can be attempted is that actual observers should set down what they have themselves observed. For there has rarely been a time when the juridical maxim that "hearsay is not evidence" ought to be more sternly insisted on.

If I now venture to set down what follows in these pages, it is because I had certain opportunities for forming a judgment at first hand for myself. I am not referring to the circumstance that for a brief period I once, long ago, lived the life of a student at a German University, or that I was frequently in Germany in the years that followed. Nor do I mean that I have tried to explore German habits of reflection, as they may be studied in the literature of Germany. Other people have done all these things more thoroughly and more extensively than I have. What I do mean is that from the end of 1905 to the summer of 1912 I had special chances for direct observation of quite another kind. During that period I was Secretary of State for War in Great Britain, and from the latter year to April, 1915, I was the holder of another office and a member of the British Cabinet.

During the first of the above periods it fell to me to work out the military organization that would be required to insure, as far as was practicable, against risk, should those strenuous efforts fail into which Sir Edward Grey, as he then was, had thrown his strength. He was endeavoring with all his might to guard the peace of Europe from danger. As he and I had for many years been on terms of close intimacy, it was not unnatural that he should ask me to do what I could by helping in some of the diplomatic work which was his, as well as by engaging in my own special task. Indeed, the two phases of activity could hardly be separable.

I was not in Germany after May, 1912, for the duties of Lord Chancellor, on which office I then entered, made it unconstitutional for me to leave the United Kingdom, save under such exceptional conditions as were conceded by the King and the Cabinet when, in the autumn of 1913, I made a brief yet memorable visit to the United States and Canada. But in 1906, while War Minister, I paid, on the invitation of the German Emperor, a visit to him at Berlin, to which city I went on after previously staying with King Edward at Marienbad, where he and the then Prime Minister, Sir Henry Campbell-Bannerman, were resting.

While at Berlin I saw much of the Emperor, and I also saw certain of his Ministers, notably Prince von Bülow, Herr von Tschirsky and General von Einem, the first being at that time Chancellor, and the last two being respectively the Foreign and War Ministers. I was invited to examine for myself the organization of the German War Office, which I wished to study for purposes of reform at home; and this I did in some detail, in company with an expert adviser from my personal staff, Colonel Ellison, my military private secretary, who accompanied me on this journey.[1] There the authorities explained to us the general nature of the organization for rapid mobilization which had been developed under the great von Moltke, and subsequently carried farther. The character of this organization was, in its general features, no secret in Germany, altho it was somewhat unfamiliar in Anglo-Saxon countries; and it interested my adviser and myself intensely.

At that time there was an active militarist party in Germany, which, of course, was not wholly pleased at the friendly reception with which we met from the Emperor and from crowds in the streets of Berlin. We were well aware of the activity of this party. But it stood then unmistakably for a minority, and I formed the opinion that those who wanted Germany to remain at peace, quite as much as to be strong, had at least an excellent chance of keeping their feet. I realized, and had done so for years past, that it was not merely because of the *beaux yeux* of foreign peoples that Germany desired to maintain good relations all round. She had become fully conscious of a growing superiority in the application to industry of scientific knowledge and in power to organize her resources founded on it; and her rulers hoped, and not without good ground, to succeed by these means in the peaceful penetration of the world.

I had personally for some time been busy in pressing the then somewhat coldly received claims for a better system of education, higher and technical as well as elementary, among my own countrymen, and had met with some success in asking for the establishment of teaching universities and of technical colleges, such as

---

[1] Of course I neither tried to obtain nor did obtain from the authorities in Germany any information that was not available to the general public there. I went simply to see the system of administration and how it was worked. Not even Count Reventlow, in his highly critical accounts of my visits in the book "Deutschlands Auswartige Politik," imagines that I had access to information which I was not free to use. The German Government had ascertained for itself that a new organization of the British Army was on foot, but it neither told its own secrets nor asked for ours.

the new Imperial College of Science and Technology at South Kensington. Of these we had very substantially increased the number during the eight years which preceded my visit to Berlin; but I had learned from visits of inspection to Germany that much more remained to be done before we could secure our commercial and industrial position against the unhasting but unresting efforts of our formidable competitor.

As to the German people outside official circles and the universities, I thought of them then what I think of them now. They were very much like our own people, except in one thing. This was that they were trained simply to obey, and to carry out whatever they were told by their rulers. I used, during numerous unofficial tours in Germany, to wander about incognito, and to smoke and drink beer with the peasants and the people whenever I could get the chance. What impressed me was the little part they had in directing their own government, and the little they knew about what it was doing. There was a general disposition to accept, as a definition of duty which must not be questioned, whatever they were told to do by the *Vorstand*. It is this habit of mind, dating back to the days of Frederick the Great, with only occasional and brief interruptions, which has led many people to think that the German people at large have in them "a double dose of original sin." Even when their soldiers have been exceptionally brutal in methods of warfare, I do not think that this is so. The habit of mind which prevails is that of always looking to the rulers for orders, and the brutality has been that enjoined — in accordance with its own military policy of shortening war by making it terrible to the enemy — by the General Staff of Germany, a body before whose injunctions even the Emperor, so far as my observation goes, always has bowed.

But I must now return to my formal visit to Berlin in the autumn of 1906. I was, as I have already said, everywhere cordially welcomed, and at the end the heads of the German Army entertained me at a dinner in the War Office, at which the War Minister presided, and there was present, among others, the Chief of the German General Staff. They were all friendly. I do not think that my impression was wrong that even the responsible heads of the Army were then looking almost entirely to "peaceful penetration," with only moral assistance from the prestige attaching to the possession of great armed forces in reserve. Our business in the United Kingdom was therefore to see that we were prepared for perils that might unexpectedly arise out of this policy, and not less, by developing our educational and industrial organization, to make ourselves fit to meet the greater likelihood of a coming keen competition in the peaceful arts.

One thing that seemed to me essential for the preservation of good relations was that cordial and frequent intercourse between the people of the two countries should be encouraged and developed. I set myself in my speeches to avoid all expressions which might be construed as suggesting a critical attitude on our part, or a failure to recognize the existence of peaceful ideas among what was then, as I still think, a large majority of the people of Germany. The attitude of some newspapers in England, and still more that of the chauvinist minority in Germany itself, did not render this quite an easy task. But there were good people in these days in Germany as well as in England, and the United States might be counted on as likely to co-operate in discouraging friction.

Meanwhile there was the chance that the course of this policy might be interrupted by some event which we could not control. A conversation with the then Chief of the German General Staff, General von Moltke, the nephew of the great man of that name, satisfied me that he did not really look with any pleasurable military expectation to the results of a war with the United Kingdom alone. It would, he observed to me, be in his opinion a long and possibly indecisive war, and must result in much of the overseas trade of both countries passing to a *tertius gaudens*, by which he meant the United States.

I had little doubt that what he said to me on this occasion represented his real opinion. But I had in my mind the apprehension of an emergency of a different nature. Germany was more likely to attack France than ourselves. The German Emperor had told me that, altho he was trying to develop good relations with France, he was finding it difficult. This seemed to me ominous. The paradox presented itself that a war with Germany in which we were alone would be easier to meet than a war in which France was attacked along with us; for if Germany succeeded in over-running France she might establish naval bases on the northern Channel ports of that country, quite close to our shores, and so, with the possible aid of the submarines, long-range guns and air-machines of the future, interfere materially with our naval position in the Channel and our fleet defenses against invasion.

I knew, too, that the French Government was apprehensive. In the historical speech which Sir Edward Grey made on August 3, 1914, the day before the British Government directed Sir Edward Goschen, our Ambassador in Berlin, to ask for his passports, he informed the House of Commons that so early as January, 1906, the French Government, after the Morocco difficulty, had drawn his attention to the international situation. It had informed him that it considered the danger of an attack on France by Germany to be a real one, and had inquired whether, in the event of an unprovoked attack, Great Britain would think that she had so much at stake as to make her willing to join in resisting it. If this were to be even a possible attitude for Great Britain, the French Government had intimated to him that it was in its opinion desirable that conversation should take place between the General Staff of France and the newly created General Staff of Great Britain, as to the form which military co-operation in resisting invasion of the northern portions of France might best assume. We had a great Navy, and the French had a great Army. But our Navy could not operate on land, and the French Army, altho large, was not so large as that which Germany, with her superior resources in population, commanded. Could we, then, reconsider our military organization, so that we might be able rapidly to dispatch, if we ever thought it necessary in our own interests, say, 100,000 men in a well-formed army, not to invade Belgium, which no one thought of doing, but to guard the French frontier of Belgium in case the German Army should seek to enter France in that way. If the German attack were made farther south, where the French chain of modern fortresses had rendered their defensive positions strong, the French Army would then be able, set free from the difficulty of mustering in full strength opposite the Belgian boundary, to guard the southern frontier.

Sir Edward Grey consulted the Prime Minister, Sir Henry Campbell-Bannerman, the Chancellor of the Exchequer, Mr. Asquith, and myself as War Minister, and I was instructed, in January, 1906, a month after assuming office, to take the examination of the question in hand. This occurred in the middle of the General Election which was then in progress. I went at once to London and summoned the heads of the British General Staff and saw the French military attaché, Colonel Huguet, a man of sense and ability. I became aware at once that there was a new army problem. It was, how to mobilize and concentrate at a place of assembly to be opposite the Belgian frontier, a force calculated as adequate (with the assistance of Russian pressure in the East) to make up for the inadequacy of the French armies for their great task of defending the entire French frontier from Dunkirk down to Belfort, or even farther south, if Italy should join the Triple Alliance in an attack.

But an investigation of a searching character presently revealed great deficiencies in the British military organization of these days. We had never contemplated the preparation of armies for warfare of the Continental type. The older generals had not been trained for this problem. We had, it was true, excellent troops in India and elsewhere. These were required as outposts for Imperial defense. As they had to serve for long periods and to be thoroughly disciplined, they had to be professional soldiers, engaged to serve in most cases for seven years with the colors and afterwards for five in the reserve. They were highly trained men, and there was a good reserve of them at home. But that reserve was not organized in the great self-contained divisions which would be required for fighting against armies organized for rapid action on modern Continental principles. Its formations in peace time were not those which would be required in such a war. There was in addition a serious defect in the artillery organization which would have prevented more than a comparatively small number of batteries (about forty-two only in point of fact) from being quickly placed on a war footing. The transport and supply and the medical services were as deficient as the artillery.

In short, the close investigation made at that time disclosed that it was not possible, under the then existing circumstances, to put in the field more than about 80,000 men, and even these only after an interval of over two months, which would be required for conversion of our isolated units into the new war formations of an army fit to take the field against the German first line of active corps. The French naturally thought that a machine so slow moving would be of little use to them. They might have been destroyed before it could begin to operate effectively. Both they and the Germans had organized on the basis that modern Continental warfare had become a high science. Hitherto we had not, and it was only our younger generals who had even studied this science.

There was, therefore, nothing for it but to attempt a complete revolution in the organization of the British Army at home. The nascent General Staff was finally organized in September, 1906, and its organization was shortly afterwards developed so as to extend to the entire Empire, as soon as a conference had taken place with the Ministers of the Dominions early in the following year. The outcome was a complete recasting, which, after three years' work, made it practicable rapidly to mobilize, not only 100,000, but 160,000 men; to transport them, with the aid of the Navy, to a place of concentration which had been settled between the staffs of France and Britain; and to have them at their appointed place within twelve days, an interval based on what the German Army required on its side for a corresponding concentration.

All the arrangements for this were worked out by the end of 1910. Both Sir John French and Sir Douglas Haig took an active part in the work. Behind the first-line army so organized, a second-line army of larger size, tho far less trained, and so designed that it could be expanded, was organized. This was the citizen or "Territorial" army, consisting in time of peace of fourteen divisions of infantry and artillery and fourteen brigades of cavalry, with the appropriate medical, sanitary, transport and other auxiliary services. Those serving in this second-line army were civilians, and, of course, much less disciplined than the officers and men of the first line. Its primary function was home defense, but its members were encouraged to undertake for service abroad, if necessary; and a large part of this army, in point of fact, fought in France, Flanders and in the East soon after the beginning of the war, in great measure making up by intelligence for shortness of training.

To say, therefore, that we were caught unprepared is not accurate. Compulsory service in a period of peace was out of the question for us. Moreover, it would have taken at least two generations to organize, and meanwhile we should have been weaker than without it. We had studied the situation and had done the only thing we thought we could do, after full deliberation. Our main strength was in our Navy and its tradition. Our secondary contribution was a small army fashioned to fulfil a scientifically measured function. It was, of course, a very small army, but it had a scientific organization on the basis of which a great expansion was possible. After all, what we set ourselves to accomplish we did accomplish. If the margin by which a just sufficient success was attained in the early days of the war seems to-day narrow, the reason of the narrow margin lay largely in the unprepared condition of the armies of Russia, on which we and France had reckoned for rapid co-operation. Anyhow, we fulfilled our contract, for at eleven o'clock on Monday morning, August 3, 1914, we mobilized without a hitch the whole of the Expeditionary Force, amounting to six divisions and nearly two cavalry divisions, and began its transport over the Channel when war was declared thirty-six hours later. We also at the same time successfully mobilized the Territorial Force and other units, the whole amounting to over half a million men. The Navy was already in its war stations, and there was no delay at all in putting what we had prepared into operation.

I speak of this with direct knowledge, for as the Prime Minister, who was holding temporarily the seals of the War Secretary, was overwhelmed with business, he asked me, tho I had then become Lord Chancellor, to go to the War Office and give directions for the mobilization of the machinery with which I was so familiar, and I did this on the morning of Monday, August 3, and a day later handed it over, in working order, to Lord Kitchener.

I now return to what was the main object of British foreign policy between 1905 and 1914, the prevention of the danger of any outbreak with Germany. Sir Edward Grey worked strenuously with this well-defined object. If France were overrun, our island security would be at least diminished, and he had, therefore, in addition to his anxiety to avert a general war, a direct national interest to strive for, in the preservation of peace between Germany and France. Ever since the mutilation which the latter country had suffered, as the outcome of the War of 1870, she had felt sore, and her relations with Germany were not easy. But she did not seek a war of revenge. It would have been too full of risk even if she had not desired peace, the Franco-Russian Dual Alliance notwithstanding. The notion of an encirclement of Germany, excepting in defense against aggression by Germany herself, existed only in the minds of nervous Germans. Still, there was suspicion, and the question was, how to get rid of it.

I have already referred to the visit I paid to the Emperor at Berlin in the autumn of 1906. He invited me to a review which he held of his troops there, and in the course of it rode up to the carriage in which I was seated and said, "A splendid machine I have in this army, Mr. Haldane; now isn't it so? And what could I do without it, situated as I am between the Russians and the French? But the French are your allies—are they not? So I beg pardon."

I shook my head and smiled deprecatingly, and replied that, were I in his Majesty's place, I should in any case feel safe from attack with the possession of this machine, and that for my own part I enjoyed being behind it much more than if I had to be in front of it.

Next day, when at the Schloss, he talked to me fully and cordially. What follows I extract from the record I made after the conversation in my diaries, which were kept by desire of King Edward, and which were printed by the Government on my return to London.

He spoke of the Anglo-French Entente. He said that it would be wrong to infer that he had any critical thought about our entente with France. On the contrary he believed that it might even facilitate good relations between France and Germany. He wished for these good relations, and was taking steps through gentlemen of high position in France to obtain them. Not one inch more of French territory would he ever covet. Alsace and Lorraine originally had been German, and now even the least German of the two, Lorraine, because it preferred a monarchy to a republic, was welcoming him enthusiastically whenever he went there. That he should have gone to Tangier, where both English and French welcomed him, was quite natural. He desired no quarrel, and the whole fault was Delcassé's, who had wanted to pick a quarrel and bring England into it.

I told the Emperor that, if he would allow me to speak my mind freely, I would do so. He assented, and I said to him that his attitude had caused great uneasiness in England, and that this, and not any notion of forming a tripartite alliance of France, Russia, and England against him, was the reason of the feeling there had been. We were bound by no military alliance. As for our entente, some time since we had difficulties with France over Newfoundland and Egypt, and we had made a good business arrangement (*gutes Geschäft*) about these complicated matters of detail, and had simply carried out our word to France.

He said that he had no criticism to make on this, except that if we had told him so early there would have been no misunderstanding. Things were better now, but we had not always been pleasant to him and ready to meet him. His army was for defense, not for offense. As to Russia, he had no Himalayas between him and Russia, more was the pity. Now what about our Two-Power standard. All this was said with earnestness, but in a friendly way, the Emperor laying his finger on my shoulder as he spoke. Sometimes the conversation was in German, but often in English.

I said that our fleet was like his Majesty's army. It was of the *Wesen* of the nation, and the Two-Power standard, while it might be rigid and so awkward, was a way of maintaining a deep-seated national tradition, and a Liberal Government must hold to it as firmly as a Conservative. Both countries were increasing in wealth—ours, like Germany, very rapidly—and if Germany built we must build. But, I added, there was an excellent opportunity for co-operation in other things. I instanced international free trade developments which would smooth other relations.

The Emperor agreed. He was convinced that free trade was the true policy for Germany also, but Germany could not go so quickly here as England had gone.

I referred to Friedrich List's great book as illustrating how military and geographical considerations had affected matters for Germany in this connection.

The Emperor then spoke of Chamberlain's policy of Tariff Reform, and said that it had caused him anxiety.

I replied that with care we might avoid any real bad feeling over trade. The undeveloped markets of the world were enormous, and we wanted no more of the surface of the globe than we had got.

The Emperor's reply was that what he sought after was not territory but trade expansion. He quoted Goethe to the effect that if a nation wanted anything it must concentrate and act from within the sphere of its concentration.

We then spoke of the fifty millions sterling per annum of chemical trade which Germany had got away from us. I said that this was thoroughly justified as the result of the practical application of high German science.

"That," said he, "I delight to think, because it is legitimate and to the credit of my people."

I agreed, and said that similarly we had got the best of the world's shipbuilding. Each nation had something to learn.

The Emperor then passed to the topic of The Hague Conference, trusting that disarmament would not be proposed. If so, he could not go in.

I observed that the word "disarmament" was perhaps unfortunately chosen.

"The best testimony," said the Emperor, "to my earnest desire for peace is that I have had no war, tho I should have had war if I had not earnestly striven to avoid it."

Throughout the conversation, which was as animated as it was long, the Emperor was cordial and agreeable. He expressed the wish that more English Ministers would visit Berlin, and that he might see more of our Royal Family. I left the Palace at 3.30 P.M., having gone there at 1.0.

On another day during this visit Prince von Bülow, who was then Chancellor, called on me. I was out, but found him later at the Schloss, and had a conversation with him. He said to me that both the Emperor and himself were thoroughly aware of the desire of King Edward and his Government to maintain the new relations with France in their integrity, and that, in the best German opinion, this was no obstacle to building up close relations with Germany also.

I said that this was the view held on our side too, and that the only danger lay in trying to force everything at once. Too great haste was to be deprecated.

He said that he entirely agreed, and quoted Prince Bismarck, who had laid it down that you can not make a flower grow any sooner by putting fire to heat it.

I said that, none the less, frequent and cordial interchanges of view were very important, and that not even the smallest matters should be neglected.

He alluded with satisfaction to my personal relations with the German Ambassador in London, Count Metternich.

I begged him, if there were any small matters which were too minute to take up officially, but which seemed unsatisfactory, to let me know of them in a private capacity through Count Metternich. This I did because I had discovered some soreness at restrictions which had been placed on the attendance of German military officers at maneuvers in England, and I had found that there had been some reprisals. I did not refer to these, but said that I had the authority of the sovereign to give assistance to German officers who were sent over to the maneuvers to study them. I added that while our army was small, compared with theirs, it had had great experience in the conduct of small expeditions, and that there were in consequence some things worth seeing.

He then spoke of the navy. It was natural that with the increase of German commerce Germany should wish to increase her fleet—from a sea-police point of view—but that they had neither the wish, nor, having regard to the strain their great army put on their resources, the power to build against Great Britain.

I said that the best opinion in England fully understood this attitude, and that we did not in the least misinterpret their recent progress, nor would he misinterpret our resolve to maintain, for purely defensive purposes, our navy at a Two-Power standard. Some day, I said, there might be rivalry, but I thought we might assume that, if it ever happened, it would not be for many years, and that our policy for the present was strongly for Free Trade, so that the more Germany exported to Great Britain and British possessions, the more we should export in exchange to them.

He expressed himself pleased that I should say this, and added that he was confident that a couple of years' interchange of friendly communications in this spirit would produce a great development, and perhaps lead for both of us to pleasant relations with other Powers also.

COUNT PAUL WOLFF METTERNICH

GERMAN AMBASSADOR TO GREAT BRITAIN FROM 1901 TO
1912.

There were during this visit in 1906 other conversations of which a record was preserved, but I have referred to the most important, and I will only mention, in concluding my account of these days in Berlin in September, 1906, the talk I had with the Foreign Minister, Herr von Tschirsky, afterward the German Ambassador at Vienna before the war, and reported as having been a fomenter of the Austrian outbreak against Serbia. He may have been anti-Slav and anti-Russian, but I did not find him, in the long conversation we had in 1906, otherwise than sensible as regards France.

I explained that my business in Berlin was merely with War Office matters, and, even as regards these, quite unofficial.

He said that there had been much tendency to misinterpret in both countries, but that things were now better. I might take it that our precision about the Entente with France, and our desire to rest firmly on the arrangement we had made, were understood in Germany, and that it was realized that we were not likely to be able to build up anything with his own country which did not rest on this basis. But he thought, and the Emperor agreed, that the Entente was no hindrance to all that was necessary between Germany and England, which was not an alliance but a thoroughly good business understanding. Some day we might come into conflict, if care were not taken; but if care was taken, there was no need of apprehension.

I said that I believed this to be Sir Edward Grey's view also, and that he was anxious to communicate with the German Government beforehand whenever there was a chance of German interests being touched.

He went on to speak of the approaching Hague Conference, and of the difficulty Germany would have if asked to alter the proportion of her army to her population—a proportion which rested on a fundamental law. For Germany alone to object to disarmament would be to put herself in a hole, and it would be a friendly act if we could devise some way out of a definite vote on reduction. Germany might well enter a conference to record and emphasize the improvement all round in international relations, the desirability of further developing this improvement, and the hope that with it the growth of armaments would cease. But he was afraid of the kind of initiative which might come from America. The United States had no sympathy with European military and naval difficulties.

I said that I thought that we, as a Government, were pledged to try to bring about something more definite than what he suggested as a limit, but that I would report what he had told me.

He then passed to general topics. He was emphatic in his assurance that what Germany wanted was increase of commercial development. Let the nations avoid inflicting pin-pricks, and leave each other free to breathe the air. He said that he thought we might have opportunities of helping them to get the French into an easier mood. They were difficult and suspicious, he observed, and it was hard to transact business with them, for they made trouble over small points.

On my return to London I sent to Herr von Tschirsky some English newspapers containing articles with a friendly tone, so far as the preservation of good relations was concerned. He replied in a letter from which I translate the material portion:

"I see with pleasure from the articles which your Excellency has sent me for his Majesty, and from other expressions of public opinion in English newspapers, that in the leading Liberal papers of England a more friendly tone toward Germany is making itself apparent. You would have been able to derive the same impression from reading our newspapers, with the exception of a few Pan-German prints. Alas! papers like *The Times, Morning Post* and *Standard* can not bring themselves to refrain from their attitude of dislike, and are always rejoicing in being suspicious of every action of the Imperial Government. They contribute in this fashion appreciably to render weak the new tone of diminishing misunderstanding which has arisen between the two countries. If I fear that under these circumstances it will be a long time before mutual understanding has grown up to the point at which it stood more than a century ago, and as you and I desire it in the well-understood interests of England and Germany, still I hope and am persuaded that the relations of the two Governments will remain good."

A year after the visit I had paid to Berlin the Emperor came over to stay with King Edward at Windsor. This was in November, 1907. The visit lasted several days, and I was present most of the time. The Emperor was accompanied by Baron von Schoen, who had become Foreign Minister of Prussia, after having been Ambassador to the Court of Russia, and by General von Einem, the War Minister, whose inclusion in the invitation I had ventured to suggest to the King, as an acknowledgment of his civility to myself as War Minister when in Berlin. There were also at Windsor Count Metternich and several high military officers of the Emperor's personal staff and military cabinet. To these officers and to the War Minister I showed all the hospitality I could in London, and I received them officially at the War Office.

But the really interesting incident of this visit, so far as I was concerned, took place at Windsor. The first evening of my visit there, just after his arrival in November, the Emperor took me aside and said he was sorry that there was a good deal of friction over the Bagdad Railway, and that he did not know what we wanted as a basis for co-operation.

I said that I could not answer for the Foreign Office, but that, speaking as War Minister, one thing I knew we wanted was a "gate" to protect India from troops coming down the new railway. He asked me what I meant by a "gate," and I said that meant the control of the section which would come near to the Persian Gulf. "I will give you the 'gate,'" replied the Emperor.

I had no opportunity at the moment, which was just before dinner, for pursuing the conversation further, but I thought the answer too important not to be followed up. There were private theatricals after dinner, which lasted till nearly one o'clock in the morning. I was seated in the theater of the Castle just behind the Emperor, and, as the company broke up, I went forward and asked him whether he really meant seriously that he was willing to give us the "gate," because, if he did mean it, I would go to London early and see Sir Edward Grey at the Foreign Office.

Next morning, about 7.30 o'clock, a helmeted guardsman, one of those whom the Emperor had brought over with him from Berlin, knocked loudly at the door and came into my bedroom, and said that he had a message from the Emperor. It was that he did mean what he had said the night before. I at once got up and caught a train for London. There I saw the Foreign Secretary, who, after taking time to think things over, gave me a memorandum he had drawn up. The substance of it was that the British Government would be very glad to discuss the Emperor's suggestion, but that it would be necessary, before making a settlement, to bring into the discussion France and Russia, whose interests also were involved. I was requested to sound the Emperor further.

After telling King Edward of what was happening, I had another conversation in Windsor Castle with the Emperor, who said that he feared that the bringing in of Russia particularly, not to speak of France, would cause difficulty; but he asked me to come that night, after a performance that was to take place in the Castle theater had ended, to his apartments, to a meeting to which he would summon the Ministers he had brought with him. He took the memorandum which I had brought from London, a copy of which I had made for him in my own handwriting, so as to present it as the informal document it was intended to be. Just before dinner Baron von Schoen spoke to me, and told me that he had heard from the Emperor what had happened, and that the Emperor was wrong in thinking that the attempt to bring in Russia would lead to difficulty, because he, Baron von Schoen, when he was Ambassador to Russia, had already discussed the general question with its Government, and had virtually come to an understanding. At the meeting that night we could therefore go on to negotiate.

I attended the Emperor in his state rooms at the Castle at one o'clock in the morning, and sat smoking with him and his Ministers for over two hours. His Foreign Minister and Count Metternich and the War Minister, von Einem, were present. I said that I felt myself an intruder, because it was very much like being present at a sitting of his Cabinet. He replied, "Be a member of my Cabinet for the evening." I said that I was quite agreeable.

They then engaged in a very animated conversation, some of them challenging the proposal of the Emperor to accept the British suggestions, with an outspokenness which would have astonished the outside world, with its notions of Teutonic autocracy. Count Metternich did not like what I suggested, that there should be a conference in Berlin on the subject of the Bagdad Railway between England, France, Russia, and Germany.

In the end, but not until after much keen argument, the idea was accepted, and the Emperor directed von Schoen to go next morning to London and make an official proposal to Sir Edward Grey, This was carried out, and the preliminary details were discussed between von Schoen and Sir Edward at the Foreign Office.

Some weeks afterward difficulties were raised from Berlin. Germany said that she was ready to discuss with the British Government the question of the terminal portion of the railway, but she did not desire to bring the other two Powers into that discussion, because the conference would probably fail and accentuate the differences between her and the other Powers.

The matter thus came to an end. It was, I think, a great pity, because I have reason to believe that the French view was that, if the Bagdad Railway question could have been settled, one great obstacle in the way of reconciling German with French and English interests would have disappeared. I came to the conclusion afterward that it was probably owing to the views of Prince von Bülow that the proposal had come to an untimely end. Whether he did not wish for an expanded entente; whether the feeling was strong in Germany that the Bagdad Railway had become a specially German concern and should not be shared; or what other reason he may have had, I do not know; but it was from Berlin, after the Emperor's return there at the end of November, 1907, that the negotiations were finally blocked.

Altho these negotiations had no definite result, they assisted in promoting increasing frankness between the two Foreign Offices, and other things went with more smoothness. Sir Edward Grey kept France and Russia informed of all we did, and he was also very open with the Germans. Until well on in 1911 all went satisfactorily. In the early part of that year the Emperor came to London to visit the present King, who had by that time succeeded to the throne. I had ventured to propose to the King that during the Emperor's visit I should, as War Minister, give a luncheon to the generals who were on his staff. But when the Emperor heard of this he sent a message that he would like to come and lunch with me himself, and to meet people whom otherwise he might not see.

I acted on my own discretion, and when he came to luncheon at my house in Queen Anne's Gate there was a somewhat widely selected party of about a dozen to meet him. For it included not only Lord Morley, Lord Kitchener, and Lord Curzon, whom he was sure to meet elsewhere, but Mr. Ramsay MacDonald, who was then leading the Labor Party, Admiral Sir Arthur Wilson, our great naval commander, Lord Moulton, Mr. Edmund Gosse, Mr. Sargent, Mr. Spender, the editor of the *Westminster Gazette*, and others representing various types of British opinion. The Emperor engaged in conversation with everyone, and all went with smoothness.

He had a great reception in London. But enthusiasm about him was somewhat damped when, in July, 1911, not long after his return to Germany, he sent the afterwards famous warship *Panther* to Agadir. The French were naturally alarmed, and the situation which had become so promising was overcast. Our naval arrangements and our new military organization were ready, and our mobilization plans were fairly complete, as the German General Staff knew from their military attaché. But the point was, how to avoid an outbreak, and to get rid of the feeling and friction to which the Agadir crisis was giving rise. Our growing good relations were temporarily clouded.

The sending of the *Panther* to Agadir was not a prudent act. It imported either too much or too little. It is said to have been the plan of Herr von Kiderlen-Waechter, at that time the Foreign Secretary and generally a sensible statesman, and to have been done in spite of misgivings expressed by the Emperor about its danger. The circumstances of the moment were such that one can not but feel a certain sympathy with the German perturbation at the time. The march of the French Army to Fez had come on them suddenly, and it at least suggested a development of French claims going beyond what Germany had agreed to at the Algeciras Conference nearly six years previously. Those who wish to inform themselves about the commotion the expedition of the French stirred up in Germany, and of the efforts the Emperor and Bethmann Hollweg had to make to restrain it, will do well to read the latter's account of what happened there in the second chapter of his recent book. But to think that the sending of a German warship could make things better was to repeat the error of judgment which had characterized "the ally in shining armor" speech of the German Emperor to Austria when she formally annexed Bosnia and Herzegovina three years before. Instead of using diplomatic methods something that looked like a threat was allowed to appear, and the answer was Mr. Lloyd George's well-known declaration of July 21, 1911, in the City of London. The sending of the *Panther*, if intelligible, was certainly unfortunate.

In the winter, after the actual crisis had been got over, there was evidence of continuing ill-feeling in Germany, and the suspicion in London did not diminish. In January, 1912, an informal message was given by the Emperor to Sir Ernest Cassel for transmission through one of my colleagues to the Foreign Office. I[2] knew nothing of this at the time, but learned shortly afterward that it was to the effect that the Emperor was concerned at the state of feeling that had arisen in both countries, and thought that the most hopeful method of improving matters would be that the Cabinet of St. James's should exchange views directly with the Cabinet of Berlin. For this course there was a good deal to be said. The peace had indeed been preserved, but, as Herr von Bethmann Hollweg told me later on, not without effort. The attitude of Germany toward France had seemed ominous. The British Government had done all it could to avert a breach, but its sympathy was opposed to language used in Germany, the spirit of which seemed to us to have in it an aggressive element. We did not hesitate to say what we thought about this.

Even after the Agadir incident was quite closed, the tension between Germany and England had not passed away. The military party in the former country began to talk of a "preventive" war pretty loudly. Even so moderate an organ in Berlin as the *Post* wrote of German opinion that "we all know that blood is assuredly about to be shed, and the longer we wait the more there will be. Few, however, have the courage to imitate Frederick the Great, and not one dares the deed."

The Emperor therefore sent his message in the beginning of 1912, to the effect that feeling had become so much excited that it was not enough to rely on the ordinary diplomatic intercourse for softening it, and that he was anxious for an exchange of views between the Cabinets of Berlin and London, of a personal and direct kind. As the result of this intimation, the British Cabinet decided to send one of its members to Berlin to hold "conversations," with a view to exploring and, if practicable, softening the causes of tension, and I was requested by the Prime Minister and Sir Edward Grey and my other colleagues to go to Berlin and undertake the task. Our Ambassador there came over to London specially to discuss arrangements, and he returned to Berlin to make them before I started.

I arrived in the German capital on February 8, 1912, and spent some days in

---

[2] This message was the response to a memorandum which Sir Ernest Cassel had brought to Berlin from some influential members of the Cabinet in London, and it contained suggestions for the improvement of the relations between the two countries. An account of Sir Ernest Cassel's visit, and of what passed when he delivered his message from London, is given in Herr von Bethmann Hollweg's recent book.

interviews with the Emperor, the Imperial Chancellor, the Naval Minister (Admiral von Tirpitz), and others of the Emperor's Ministry. The narrative of my conversations I have extracted from the records I made after each interview, for the preservation so far as possible of the actual expressions used during it.

My first interview was one with Herr von Bethmann Hollweg, the Imperial Chancellor. We met in the British Embassy, and the conversation, which was quite informal, was a full and agreeable one. My impression, and I still retain it, was that Bethmann Hollweg was then as sincerely desirous of avoiding war as I was myself. I told him of certain dangers quite frankly, and he listened and replied with what seemed to me to be a full understanding of our position. I said that the increasing action of Germany in piling up magnificent armaments was, of course, within the unfettered rights of the German people. But the policy had an inevitable consequence in the drawing together of other nations in the interests of their own security. This was what was happening. I told him frankly that we had made naval and military preparations, but only such as defense required, and as would be considered in Germany matter of routine. I went on to observe that our faces were set against aggression by any nation, and I told him, what seemed to relieve his mind, that we had no secret military treaties. But, I added, if France were attacked and an attempt made to occupy her territory, our neutrality must not be reckoned on by Germany. For one thing, it was obvious that our position as an island protected by the sea would be affected seriously if Germany had possession of the Channel ports on the northern shores of France. Again, we were under treaty obligation to come to the aid of Belgium in case of invasion, just as we were bound to defend Portugal and Japan in certain eventualities. In the third place, owing to our dependence on freedom of sea-communications for food and raw materials, we could not sit still if Germany elected to develop her fleet to such an extent as to imperil our naval protection. She might build more ships, but we should in that case lay down two keels for each one she laid down.

The Chancellor said that he did not take my observations at all in bad part, but I must understand that his admirals and generals were pretty difficult.

I replied that the difficulty would be felt at least as much with the admirals and generals in my own country.

The Chancellor, in the course of our talk, proposed a formula of neutrality to which I will refer later on.

I left the Chancellor with the sense that I had been talking with an honest man struggling somewhat with adversity. However, next day I was summoned to luncheon with the Emperor and Empress at the Schloss, and afterward had a long interview, which lasted nearly three hours, with the Emperor and Admiral von Tirpitz in the Emperor's cabinet room. The conversation was mainly in German, and was confined to naval questions. My reception by the Emperor was very agreeable; that by Tirpitz seemed to me a little strained. The question was, whether Germany must not continue her program for expanding her fleet. What that program really amounted to we had not known in London, except that it included an increase in battleships; but the Emperor handed me at this meeting a confidential copy of the draft of the proposed new Fleet Law, with an intimation that he had no objection to my communicating it privately to my colleagues. I was careful to abstain even from looking at it then, for I saw that, from its complexity and bulk, it would require careful study. So I simply put it in my pocket. But I repeated what I had said to the Chancellor, that the necessity for secure sea-communications rendered it vital for us to be able to protect ourselves on the seas. Germany was quite free to do as she pleased, but so were we, and we should probably lay down two keels for every one which she added to her program. The initiative in slackening competition was really not with us, but with Germany. Any agreement for settling our differences and introducing a new spirit into the relations of the two nations would be bones without flesh if Germany began by fresh shipbuilding, and so forced us to do twice as much. Indeed, the world would laugh at such an agreement, and our people would think that we had been fooled. I did not myself take that view, because I thought that the mere fact of an agreement was valuable. But the Emperor would see that the public would attach very little importance to his action unless the agreement largely modified what it believed to be his shipbuilding program.

We then discussed the proposal of the German Admiralty for the new program. Admiral von Tirpitz struggled for it. I insisted that fundamental modification was essential if better relations were to ensue. The tone was friendly, but I felt that I was up against the crucial part of my task. The admiral wanted us to enter into some understanding about our own shipbuilding. He thought the Two-Power standard a hard one for Germany, and, indeed, Germany could not make any admission about it.

I said it was not matter for admission. They were free and so were we, and we must for the sake of our safety remain so. The idea then occurred to us that, as we should never agree about it, we should avoid trying to define a standard proportion in any general agreement that we might come to, and, indeed, say nothing in it about shipbuilding; but that the Emperor should announce to the German public that the agreement on general questions, if we should have concluded one, had entirely modified his wish for the new Fleet Law, as originally conceived, and that it should be delayed, and future shipbuilding should at least be spread over a longer period.

The Emperor thought such an agreement would certainly make a great difference, and he informed me that his Chancellor would propose to me a formula as a basis for it. I said that I would see the Chancellor and discuss a possible formula, as well as territorial and other questions with him, and would then return to London and report to the King (from whom I had brought him a special and friendly message) and to my colleagues the good disposition I had found, and leave the difficulties about shipbuilding and indeed all other matters to their judgment. For I had come to Berlin, not to make an actual agreement, but only to explore the ground for one with the Emperor and his ministers. I had been struck with the friendly disposition in Berlin, and a not less friendly disposition would be found in London.

The evening after my interview with the Emperor I dined with the Chancellor.

I met there and talked with several prominent politicians, soldiers, and men of letters, including Kiderlen-Waechter (the then Foreign Secretary), the afterward famous General von Hindenburg, Zimmermann of the Foreign Office, and Professor Harnack.

Later on, after dinner, I went off to meet the French Ambassador, M. Jules Cambon, at the British Embassy, for I wished to keep him informed of our object, which was simply to improve the state of feeling between London and Berlin, but on the basis, and only on the basis, of complete loyalty to our Entente with France. It was, to use a phrase which he himself suggested in our conversation, a *détente* rather than an *entente* that I had in view, with possible developments to follow it which might assume a form which would be advantageous to France and Russia, as well as to ourselves and Germany. He showed me next day the report of our talk which he had prepared in order to telegraph it to Paris.

I had other interviews the next day, but the only one which is important for the purposes of the present narrative is that at my final meeting with the German Chancellor on the Saturday (February 10). I pressed on him how important it was for public opinion and the peace of the world that Germany should not force us into a shipbuilding competition with her, a competition in which it was certain that we should have to spare no effort to preserve our margin of safety by greater increases.

He did not controvert my suggestion. I could see that personally he was of the same mind. But he said that the forces he had to contend with were almost insuperable. The question of a retardation of building under the proposed Fleet Law was not susceptible of being treated apart from that of the formula of which he and the Emperor had both spoken. He suggested that we might agree on the following formula:

1. The High Contracting Powers assure each other mutually of their desire for peace and friendship.

2. They will not, either of them, make any combination, or join in any combination, which is directed against the other. They expressly declare that they are not bound by any such combination.

3. If either of the High Contracting Parties become entangled in a war with one or more other powers, the other of the High Contracting Parties will at least observe toward the power so entangled a benevolent neutrality, and use its utmost endeavor for the localization of the conflict.

4. The duty of neutrality which arises from the preceding article has no application in so far as it may not be reconcilable with existing agreements which the High Contracting Parties have already made. The making of new agreements which make it impossible for either of the Contracting Parties to observe neutrality toward the other beyond what is provided by the preceding limitations is excluded in conformity with the provisions contained in Article 2.

M. PAUL CAMBON

FRENCH AMBASSADOR TO GREAT BRITAIN SINCE 1898.

Anxious as I was to agree with the Chancellor, who seemed as keen as I was to meet me with expressions which I might take back to England for friendly consideration, I was unable to hold out to him the least prospect that we could accept the draft formula which he had just proposed. Under Article 2, for example, we should find ourselves, were it accepted, precluded from coming to the assistance of France should Germany attack her and aim at getting possession of such ports as Dunkirk, Calais, and Boulogne, a friendly occupation of which was so important for our island security. Difficulties might also arise which would hamper us in the discharge of our existing treaty obligations to Belgium, Portugal, and Japan. The most hopeful way out was to revise the draft fundamentally by confining its terms to an undertaking by each Power not to make any unprovoked attack upon the other, or join in any combination or design against the other for purposes of aggression, or become party to any plan or naval or military combination, alone or in conjunction with any other Power, directed to such an end.

He and I then sat down and redrafted what he had prepared, on this basis, but without his committing himself to the view that it would be sufficient. We also had a satisfactory conversation about the Bagdad Railway and other things in Turkey connected with the Persian Gulf, and we discussed possibilities of the rearrangement of certain interests of both Powers in Africa. He said to me that he was not there to make any immediate bargain, but that we should look at the African question on both sides from a high point of view, and that if we had any difficulties we should tell him, and he would see whether he could get round them for us.

I replied that I also was not there to make a bargain, but only to explore the ground, and that I much appreciated the tone of his conversation with me, and the good feeling he had shown. I should go back to London and without delay report to my colleagues all that had passed.

I entertain no doubt that the German Chancellor was sincerely in earnest in what he said to me on these occasions, and in his desire to improve relations with us and keep the peace. So I think was the Emperor; but he was pulled at by his naval and military advisers, and by the powerful, if then small, chauvinist party in Germany. In 1912, when the conversations recorded took place, this party was less potent, I think a good deal less, than it appears to have become a year and a half later, when Germany had increased her army still further. But I formed the opinion even then that the power of the Emperor in Germany was a good deal misinterpreted and overestimated. My impression was that the really decisive influence was that of the Minister who had managed to secure the strongest following throughout Germany; and it was obvious to me that Admiral von Tirpitz had a powerful and growing following from many directions, due to the backing of the naval party.

Moreover, sensible as a large number of Germans were, there was a certain tendency to swelled-headedness in the nation. It had had an extraordinarily rapid development, based on principles of organization in every sphere of activity—principles derived from the lesson of the necessity of thinking before acting enjoined by the great teachers of the beginning of the nineteenth century. The period down to about 1832 seems to me to correspond, in the intellectual prodigies it produced, to our Elizabethan period. It came no doubt to an end in its old and distinctive aspect. But its spirit assumed, later on, a new form, that of organization for material ends based on careful reflection and calculation. In industry, in commerce, in the army, and in the navy, the work of mind was everywhere apparent. *"Aus einem Lernvolk wollen wir ein Thatvolk werden"* was the new watchword.

No doubt there was much that was defective. When it came to actual war in 1914, it turned out that Germany had not adequately thought out her military problems. If she had done so, she would have used her fleet at the very outset, and particularly her destroyers and submarines, to try to hinder the transport of the British Expeditionary Force to France, and, having secured the absence of this force, she would have sought to seize the northern ports of France. Small as the Expeditionary Force was, it was enough, when added to the French armies, to make them so formidable as to render the success of von Kluck uncertain if the troops could be concentrated to resist him swiftly enough. Again, Germany never really grasped the implications of our command of the sea. Had she done so, I do not think she would have adventured war. She may have counted on England not coming in, owing to entanglements in Irish difficulties. If so, this was just another instance of her bad judgment about the internal affairs of other nations.

In fine, Germany had not adequately thought out or prepared for the perils which she undertook when she assumed the risks of the war of 1914. No doubt she knew more about the shortcomings of the Russian army than did the French or the British. On these, pretty exact knowledge of the Russian shortages enabled her to reckon. There we miscalculated more than she did. But she was not strong enough to make sure work of a brief but conclusive campaign in the West, which was all she could afford while Russia was organizing. Then, later on, she ought to have seen that, if the submarine campaign which she undertook should bring the United States into the war, her ultimate fate would be sealed by blockade. In the end she no doubt fought magnificently. But she made these mistakes, which were mainly due to that swelled-headedness which deflected her reasoning and prevented her from calculating consequences aright.

There was a good deal of this apparent even in 1912. It had led to the Agadir business in the previous summer, and the absence of wise prevision was still apparent. I believed that this phase of militarism would pass when Imperial Germany became a more mature nation. Indeed, it was passing under the growing influence of Social Democracy, which was greatly increased by the elections which took place while I was in Berlin in 1912. But[3] still there was the possibility of an explosion; and when I returned to London, altho I was full of hope that relations between the two countries were going to be improved, and told my colleagues so, I also reported that there were three matters about which I was uneasy.

The first was my strong impression that the new Fleet Law would be insisted on.

The second was the possibility that Tirpitz might be made Chancellor of the Empire in place of Bethmann Hollweg. This was being talked of as possible when I was in Berlin.

[3] An anecdote illustrating the change that was coming over political opinion in Germany in 1912, may be worth relating. I was present at a supper party, given by one of the professors in a well-known German University town, in May of that year. I asked him whether the old Conservative member who had for long represented the town had been again returned. "Returned! no," he replied. "It was impossible to return a man of moderate opinions. We only escaped a Social Democrat by a few votes. We managed to get enough of the popular vote to return a fairly sensible railway servant for this University town." I inquired what party he belonged to. "No old party," was his answer, and it will interest you to know that his program was an English one: *"Lloyd Georgianismus."* I then inquired what was his text book. *"Die Reden von Lloyd George,"* was the answer. Did it contain anything about a place called Limehouse? *"Limhaus, ach ja; das war eine vortreffliche Rede!"*

The third was the want of continuity in the supreme direction of German policy. Foreign policy especially was under divided control. Von Tschirsky observed to me in 1906 that what he had been saying about a question we were discussing represented his view as Foreign Minister of Prussia, but that next door was the Chancellor, who might express quite a different view to me if I asked him; and that if, later on, I went to the end of the Wilhelmstrasse and turned down Unter den Linden I would come to the Schloss, where I might derive from the Emperor's lips an impression quite different from that given by either himself or the Chancellor. This made me feel that, desirous as Bethmann Hollweg had shown himself to establish and preserve good relations, we could not count on his influence being maintained or prevailing. As an eminent foreign diplomatist observed, "In this highly organized nation, when you have ascended to the very top story you find not only confusion but chaos."

However, after I had reported fully on all the details and the Foreign Office had received my written report, matters were taken in hand by Sir Edward Grey, and by him I was kept informed. Presently it became apparent that there were those in Berlin who were interfering with the Chancellor in his efforts for good relations. A dispatch came which was inconsistent with the line he had pursued with me, and it became evident that the German Government was likely to insist on proceeding with the new Fleet Law. When we looked closely into the copy of the draft which the Emperor had given to me, we found very large increases contemplated, of which we had no notion earlier, not only in the battleships, about which we did know before, but in small craft and submarines and personnel. As these increases were to proceed further, discussion about the terms of a formula became rather futile, and we had only one course left open to us—to respond by quietly increasing our navy and concentrating its strength in northern seas. This was done with great energy by Mr. Churchill, the result being that, as the outcome of the successive administrations of the fleet by Mr. McKenna and himself, the estimates were raised by over twenty millions sterling to fifty-one millions.

In the summer of 1912 I became Lord Chancellor, and the engrossing duties, judicial as well as administrative, of that office cut me off from any direct participation in the carrying on of our efforts for better relations with Germany. But these relations continued to be extended in the various ways practicable and left open to Sir Edward Grey and the German Chancellor. The discussions which had been begun when I was in Berlin, about Africa and the Bagdad Railway, were continued between them through the Ambassadors; and just before the war the draft of an extensive treaty had been agreed on.

Then, after an interval of two years, came a time of extreme anxiety. No one had better opportunities than I of watching Sir Edward's concentration of effort to avoid the calamity which threatened. For he was living with me in my house in Queen Anne's Gate through the whole of these weeks, and he was devoting himself, with passionate earnestness of purpose, to inducing the German Government to use its influence with Austria for a peaceful settlement. But it presently became evident that the Emperor and his Ministers had made up their minds that they were going to make use of an opportunity that appeared to have come. As I have already said, I think their calculations were framed on a wholly erroneous basis. It is clear that their military advisers had failed to take account, in their estimates of probabilities, of the tremendous moral forces that might be brought into action against them. The ultimate result we all know. May the lesson taught to the world by the determined entry of the United States into the conflict between right and wrong never be forgotten by the world!

International

VISCOUNT GREY OF FALLODON
SECRETARY OF STATE FOR FOREIGN AFFAIRS FROM 1905
TO 1916.

Why Germany acted as she did then is a matter that still requires careful investigation. My own feeling is that she has demonstrated the extreme risk of confiding great political decisions to military advisers. It is not their business to have the last word in deciding between peace and war. The problem is too far-reaching for their training. Bismarck knew this well, and often said it, as students of his life and reflections are aware. Had he been at the helm I do not believe that he would have allowed his country to drift into a disastrous course. He was far from perfect in his ethical standards, but he had something of that quality which Mommsen, in his history, attributes to Julius Cæsar. Him the historian describes as one of those "mighty ones who has preserved to the end of his career the statesman's tact of discriminating between the possible and the impossible, and has not broken down in the task which for greatly gifted natures is the most difficult of all—the task of recognizing, when on the pinnacle of success, its natural limits. What was possible he performed, and never left the possible good undone for the sake of the impossible better; never disdained at least to mitigate by palliatives evils that were incurable. But where he recognized that fate had spoken, he always obeyed. Alexander on the Hypanis, Napoleon at Moscow, turned back because they were compelled to do so, and were indignant at destiny for bestowing even on its favorites merely limited successes. Cæsar turned back voluntarily on the Thames and on the Rhine, and thought of carrying into effect even at the Danube and the Euphrates, not unbounded plans of world-conquest, but merely well-considered frontier regulations."

If only Germany, whose great historian thus explained these things, had remembered them, how different might have been her position to-day. But it may be that she had carried her policy too far to be left free. With her certainly rests the main responsibility for what has happened; for apart from her, Austria would not have acted as she did, nor would Turkey, nor Bulgaria. The fascinating glitter of her armies, and the assurances given by her General Staff, were too much for the minor nations whom she had induced to accept her guidance, and too much I think also for her own people. No doubt the ignorance of these about the ways of their own Government counted for a great deal. There has never been such a justification of the principle of democratic control as this war affords. But a nation must be held responsible for the action of its own rulers, however much it has simply submitted itself to them. I have the impression that even to-day in its misery the German public does not fully understand, and still believes that Germany was the victim of a plot to entrap and encircle her, and that with this in view Russia mobilized on a great scale for war. It is difficult for us to understand how real the Slav peril appeared to Germany and to Austria, and there is little doubt that to the latter Serbia was an unquiet neighbor. But these considerations must be taken in their context—a context of which the German public ought to have made itself fully aware. The leaders of its opinion were bent on domination to the Near East. No wonder that the Slavs in the Balkan Peninsula became progressively alarmed, and looked to Russia more and more for protection. For it had become plain that moral considerations would not be allowed by the authorities at Berlin to weigh in the balance against material advantages to be gained by power of domination.

If there is room for reproach to us Anglo-Saxons, it is reproach of a very different kind. Germany was quite intelligent enough to listen to reason, and, besides, she had the prospect of becoming the dominating industrial and commercial power in the world by dint merely of peaceful penetration. It is possible that, if her relations with her Western neighbors, including Great Britain, had been more intimate than they actually were, she might have been saved from a great blunder, and might have come to understand that the English-speaking races were not really so inferior to herself as she took them to be. Her *hubris* was in part, at all events, the result of ignorance. Speaking for my own countrymen, I think that neither did we know enough about the Germans nor did the Germans know enough about us. They were ignorant of the innate capacity for fighting, in industrial and military conflicts alike, which our history shows we have always hitherto brought to light in great emergencies. And they little realized how tremendously moral issues could stir and unite democracies. We, on the other hand, knew little of their tradition, their literature, or their philosophy. Our statesmen did not read their newspapers, and rarely visited their country. We were deficient in that quality which President Murray Butler has spoken of as the "international mind."

I do not know whether, had it been otherwise, we could have brought about the better state of things in Europe for which I tried to express the hope, altho not without misgiving, in the address on "Higher Nationality" which I was privileged to deliver before distinguished representatives of the United States and of Canada at Montreal on September 1, 1913. I spoke then of the possibility of a larger entente, an entente which might become a real concert of the Great Powers of the world; and I quoted the great prayer with which Grotius concludes his book on "War and Peace." There was at least the chance, if we strove hard enough, that we might find a response from the best in other countries, and in the end attain to a new and real *Sittlichkeit* which should provide a firmer basis for International Law and reverence for international obligations. But for the realization of this dream a sustained and strenuous search after fuller mutual knowledge was required.

After this address had been published, I received a letter from the German Chancellor, Bethmann Hollweg, in which—writing in German and so late as September 26, 1913—he expressed himself to me as follows:

> "If I had the happiness of finding myself in one mind with you in these thoughts in February, 1912, it has been to me a still greater satisfaction that our two countries have since then had a number of opportunities of working together in this spirit. Like you, I hold the optimistic view that the great nations will be able to progress further on this path, and will do so. Anyhow, I shall, in so far as it is within my power, devote my energies to this cause, and I am happy in the certainty of finding in you an openly declared fellow-worker."

But events swept him from a course which, so far as I know, he at least individually desired to follow. The great increase of armaments took place that year in Germany, and, when events were too strong for him, he elected, not to resign, but to throw in his lot with his country. His position was one of great difficulty. He took a course for which many would applaud him. But inherently a wrong course, surely. What he said when Belgium was invaded in breach of solemn treaty shows that he felt this. He let himself be swept into devoting his energies to bolstering up his country's cause, instead of resigning. His career only proves that, given the political conditions that obtained in Germany shortly before the war, it was almost impossible for a German statesman to keep his feet or to avoid being untrue to himself. And yet there were many others there in the same frame of mind, and one asks oneself whether, had they had more material to work with, they might not have been able to present a more attractive alternative than the notion of military domination which in the end took possession of all, from the Emperor downward.

It is, however, useless to speculate at present on these things. We know too little of the facts. The historians of another generation will know more. But of one thing I feel sure. The Germans think that Great Britain declared war of pre-conceived purpose and her own initiative. There is a sense in which she did. The opinion of Mr. Asquith, Sir Edward Grey, and of those of us who were by their side, was unhesitating. She could not have taken any other course than she did without the prospect of ruin and failure to enter on the only path of honor. For honor and safety alike necessitated that she should take, without the delay which would have been fatal, the step she did take without delay and unswervingly. The responsibility for her entry comes back wholly to Germany herself, who would not have brought it about had she not plunged into war. And to-day Germany lies prostrate.

But she is not dead. I do not think that for generations to come she will dream of building again on military foundations. Her people have had a lesson in the overwhelming forces which are inevitably called into action where there is brutal indifference to the moral rights of others. What remains to her is that which she has inherited and preserved of the results of the great advancement in knowledge which began under the inspiration of Lessing and Kant, and culminated in the teaching of Goethe and Schiller and of the thinkers who were their contemporaries. That movement only came to a partial end in 1832. No doubt its character changed after that. The idealists in poetry, music, and philosophy gave place to great men of science, to figures such as those of Ludwig and Liebig, of Gauss, Riemann, and Helmholtz. There came also historians like Ranke and Mommsen, musicians like Wagner, philosophers like Schopenhauer and Lotze, a statesman like Bismarck. To-day there are few men of great stature in Germany; there are, indeed, few men of genius anywhere in the world. But Germany still has a high general level in science, and of recent years she has produced great captains of industry. The gift for organization founded on principle, and for applying science to practical uses, was there before the war, and it is very unsafe to assume that it is not there in a latent form to-day. If it is, Germany will be heard of again with a field of activity that probably will not include devotion to military affairs in the old way. Against her competition of this other kind, formidable as soon as she has recovered from her misery, we must prepare ourselves in the only way that can succeed in the long run. We, too, must study and organize on the basis of widely diffused exact knowledge, and not less of high ethical standards. I think, if I read the signs of the times aright, that people are coming to realize this, both in the United States and throughout the British Empire.

Press Illustrating Service

CHANCELLOR THEOBALD VON BETHMANN-HOLLWEG

CHANCELLOR OF THE GERMAN EMPIRE AND MINISTER
OF STATE FOR FOREIGN AFFAIRS
FROM 1909 TO 1917.

CHAPTER III

THE GERMAN ATTITUDE BEFORE THE WAR

We now have before us the considered opinions of Herr von Bethmann Holl-weg, the late Imperial Chancellor, and of Admiral von Tirpitz, the Minister who did much to develop the naval power of Germany, about the origin and significance of the war. Both have written books on the subject. It is[4] to be desired that in the case of each of these authors his book should be studied in English-speaking countries as well as on the Continent. For it is important that the Anglo-Saxon world should understand the divergences in policy which the two books disclose, not less than the points of agreement. That world has suffered in the past from failure to understand Germany, while the German world has displayed a total inability to interpret aright the Anglo-Saxon disposition. When I speak of two worlds I mean the governing classes of these worlds. The nations themselves, taken as aggregates of individual citizens, by a probable majority in each case, desired the continuance of peace and of the prosperity of which it is the condition. So, of course, did the rulers, those in Germany as much as those in London. But the German rulers had a theory of how to secure peace which was the outcome of the abstract mind that was their inheritance. It was the theory that was wrong, a theory of which Anglo-Saxondom knew little, and which it would have rejected decisively had it realized its tendency. This theory is described in Admiral Tirpitz's book, with an account of the efforts made to indoctrinate with it the people of Germany.

The two volumes are profoundly interesting. For in that of Admiral Tirpitz we have the doctrine set forth that in the end led to the war. In that written by the late Imperial Chancellor we have quite another principle laid down as the one which he was endeavoring to apply in his direction of German policy. But in this endeavor he failed. The school of Tirpitz in the main prevailed, and this was the more easy, inasmuch as it was simply continuing the policy which had been advocated by a noisy section of Germans, nearly without a break, since the days of Frederick the Great. It was a policy which had in reality outlived the days in which it was practicable. The world had become too crowded and too small to permit of any one Power asserting its right to jostle its way where it pleased without regard to its neighbors. An affair of police on a colossal scale had begun to look as if it would ensue, and ensue it ultimately did. No doubt had we all been cleverer we might have been able to explain to Germany whither she was heading. But we

---

[4] "Betrachtungen zum Weltkriege," Th. von Bethmann Hollweg. "Erinnerungen," Alfred von Tirpitz. Both translated into English under the Titles: "Reflections on the World War," and "My Memoirs."

did not understand her, least of all our chauvinists, nor did she understand us. In the main what she really wanted was to develop herself by the application of her talent for commerce and industry. To her success in attaining this end we had no objection, provided her procedure was decent and in order. But she chose a means to her end which was becoming progressively more and more inadmissible. Tirpitz describes the illegitimate *means*. Bethmann Hollweg describes the legitimate *end*. Tirpitz thinks Bethmann Hollweg was a weakling because he would not back up the means. Bethmann Hollweg, firm in his faith that the end was legitimate and thinking of this alone, dwells on it with little reference to what his colleague was about. His accusation against the Entente Powers is that, at the instigation of Russia primarily, and in a less degree of France, they set themselves to ring round and crush Germany. It was really, he believes, a war of aggression, and England was ultimately responsible for it. Without her co-operation it was impossible, and altho she did not enter into any formal military alliance for the purpose, she began in the time of Edward VII. a policy of close friendship which enabled Russia and France in the end to reckon on her as morally bound to help. It was easy for these Powers to represent as a defensive war what was really a war of aggression. Such was truly its nature, and England decided to join in it, actually because she was jealous of Germany's growing success in the world, and was desirous of setting a check to it.

Such is Herr von Bethmann Hollweg's explanation. He is, I have no doubt, sincerely convinced of its truth, and he explains the grounds of his conviction in detail and with much ability. But there is a fallacy in his reasoning which becomes transparent when one reads along with his book that of his colleague. If we put out of sight the deep feeling awakened here by the brutality of the invasion of Belgium, to which violation of Treaty obligations the former declares that Germany was compelled by military considerations that were unanswerable, and look at the history of Anglo-German relations before the war, the inference is irresistible that it was not the object of developing in a peaceful atmosphere German commerce and industry that England objected to. Such a development might have been formidable for us. It would have compelled great efforts on our part to improve the education of our people and our organization for peaceful enterprises. But it would have been legitimate. The objection of this country was directed against quite other things that were being done by Germany in order to attain her purpose. The essence of these was the attempt to get her way by creating armaments which should in effect place her neighbors at her mercy. We who live on islands, and are dependent for our food and our raw materials on our being able to protect their transport and with it ourselves from invasion, could not permit the sea-protection which had been recognized from generation to generation as a necessity for our preservation to be threatened by the creation of naval forces intended to make it precarious. As the navies of Europe were growing, not only those of France and Russia, but the navy of Italy also, we had to look, in the interests of our security, to friendly relations with these countries. We aimed at establishing such friendly relations, and our method was to get rid of all causes of friction, in Newfoundland, in Egypt, in the East, and in the Mediterranean. That was the policy which was implied in our Ententes. We were not willing to enter into military alliances and we did not do so. Our policy was purely a business policy, and everything else was consequential on this, including the growing sense of common interests and of the desire for the maintenance of peace. I do not think that Admiral Tirpitz wanted actual war. But he did want power to enforce submission to the expansion of Germany at her will. And this power was his means to the end which was what less Prussianized minds in Germany contemplated as attainable in less objectionable ways. Such a means he could not fashion in the form of strength in sea power which would have placed us at his mercy, without arousing our instinct for self-preservation.

All this the late Imperial Chancellor in substance ignores. The fact is that he can only defend his theory on the hypothesis that no such policy as that of his colleague was on foot, and that the truth was that France, Russia, and England had come to a decision to take the initiative in a policy embracing, for France revenge for the loss of Alsace and Lorraine, for Russia the acquisition of Constantinople with domination over the Balkans and the Bosporus, and for England the destruction of German commerce. If this hypothesis be not true, and the real explanation of the alarm of the Entente Powers was the policy exemplified by Tirpitz and the other exponents of German militarism, then the whole of the reasoning in Herr von Bethmann Hollweg's book falls to the ground.

It may be asked how it was possible that two members of the Imperial Government should have been pursuing in the same period two policies wholly inconsistent with each other. The answer is not difficult. The direction of affairs in Germany was admirably organized for some purposes and very badly for others. Her autocratic system lent itself to efficiency in the preparation of armaments. But it was not really a system under which her Emperor was left free to guide policy. There is no greater mistake made than that under which it is popularly supposed that the Emperor was absolute master. The development in recent years of the influence of the General and Admiral Staffs, which was a necessity from the point of view of modern organization for war but required keeping in careful check from other points of view, had produced forces which the Emperor was powerless to hold in. Even in Bismarck's time readers of his "Reflections and Recollections" will remember how he felt the embarrassment of his foreign policy caused by the growing and deflecting influences of Moltke, and even of his friend Roon. And there was no Bismarck to hold the Staffs in check for reasons of expediency in the years before 1914. The military mind when it is highly developed is dangerous. It sees only its own bit, but this it sees with great clearness, and in consequence becomes very powerful. There is only one way of holding it to its legitimate function, and that is by the supremacy of public opinion in a Parliament as its final exponent. Parliaments may be clumsy and at times ignorant. But they do express, it may be vaguely, but yet sufficiently, the sense of the people at large. Now, notwithstanding all that had been done to educate them up to it, I do not think that the people at large in Germany had ever endorsed the implications of the policy of German militarism. The Social Democrats certainly had not. They ought, I think, to be judged even now by what they said before the war, and not by what some, tho not all of them, said when it was pressed on them in 1914 that Germany had to fight for her life. Had she possessed a true Parliamentary system for a generation before the war there would probably have been no war. What has happened to her is a vindication of Democracy as the best political system despite certain drawbacks which attach to it.

The great defect of the German Imperial system was that, unless the Emperor was strong enough to impose his will on his advisers, he was largely at their mercy. Had they been chosen by the people, the people and not the Emperor would have borne the responsibility, if the views of these advisers diverged from their own. But they were chosen by the Emperor, and chosen in varying moods as to policy. The result was that, excellent as were the departments at their special work in most cases, on general policy there was no guarantee for unity of mind. The Emperor lived amid a sea of conflicting opinions. The Chancellor might have one idea, the Foreign Secretary, a Prussian and not Imperial Minister, a different one, the Chief of the General Staff a third, the War Minister a fourth, and the Head of the Admiralty a fifth. Thus the Kaiser was constantly being pulled at from different sides, and whichever Minister had the most powerful combination at his back generally got the best of the argument. Were the Kaiser in an impulsive mood he might side now with one and again with another, and the result would necessarily be confusion. Moreover, he had constantly to fix one eye on public opinion in Germany, and another on public opinion abroad. It is therefore not surprising that Germany seemed to foreigners a strange and unintelligible country, and that sudden manifestations of policy were made which shocked us here, accustomed as we were to something quite different. Neither our pacifists nor our chauvinists really succeeded in diagnosing Germany. On the other hand, we ourselves were a standing puzzle to the Germans. They could not understand how Government could be conducted in the absence of abstract principles exactly laid down. And because our democratic system was one of choosing our rulers and trusting them with a large discretion within limits, the Germans always suspected that this system, with which they were unfamiliar, covered a device for concealing hidden policies. I wrote in some detail about this in an address delivered at Oxford in the autumn of 1911, and afterward published in a little volume called "Universities and National Life."

The war has not altered the views to which I had then come.

But it was not really so on either side, and it is deplorable that the two nations knew so little of each other. For I believe that the German system, wholly unadapted as it was to the modern spirit, was bound to become modified before long, and had we shown more skill and more zeal in explaining ourselves, we should probably have accelerated the process of German acceptance of the true tendencies of the age. But our statesmen took little trouble to get first-hand knowledge of the genesis of what appeared to them to be the German double dose of original sin, and, on the other hand, our chauvinists were studied in Germany out of all proportion to their small number and influence. Thus the Berlin politicians got the wrong notions to which their tradition predisposed them. I believe that Herr von Bethmann Hollweg was himself really more enlightened, but he could not control the admirals and generals, or the economists or historians or professors whom the admirals and generals were always trying to enlist on the side of the doctrine of *Weltmacht oder Niedergang*. Under these circumstances all that seemed possible was to try to influence German opinion, and at the same time to insure against the real risk of failure to accomplish this before it was too late.

In order to make this view of German conditions intelligible, it will be convenient in the first place to give some account of Herr von Bethmann Hollweg's opinions as expressed in his book, and afterward to contrast them with the views of his powerful colleague, Admiral von Tirpitz.

The ex-Imperial Chancellor commences his *"Betrachtungen zum Weltkriege"* by going back to the day when he assumed office. When Prince Bülow handed over the reins to him in July, 1909, the Prince gave him his views on what, in the attitude of England, had been causing the former much concern. We are not told what he actually said, but we can guess it, for Bethmann Hollweg goes on to indicate the origin of the cause of anxiety. It was King Edward's "encirclement" policy. It might well be that the late King had no desire for war. But the result of the policy for which he and the Ministers behind him stood was, so he believes, that, in all differences of opinion as to external policy, Germany found England, France, and Russia solidly against her, and was conscious of a continuous attempt to lead Italy away from the Triple Alliance. "People may call this *'Einkreisung,'* or policy of the balance of power, or whatever they like. The object and the achievement resulted in the founding of a group of nations of great power, whose purpose was to hinder Germany at least by diplomatic means in the free development of her growing strength." Sir Edward Grey, when taking over the conduct of foreign policy in 1905, had declared that he would continue the policy of the late Government. He hoped for improved relations with Russia, and even for more satisfactory relations with Germany, provided always that in the latter case these did not interfere with the friendship between England and France. This, says Bethmann Hollweg, had been the theme of English policy since the end of the days of "splendid isolation," and it remained so until the war broke out. He says nothing of the rapid advances which were proceeding from stage to stage in the organization of German battle-fleets to be added to her formidable army, or of the risk these advances made for England if she were to find herself without any friends outside.

As regards Russia, Isvolsky, who had never forgiven the Austrian Foreign Minister, Count d'Aerenthal, for his diplomatic victory in getting the annexation to Austria of Bosnia and Herzegovina in 1908, was very hostile to Austria, and consequently to her Ally. In the case of France, again, it was indeed true that M. Jules Cambon had repeatedly emphasized to the ex-Chancellor the desire for more intimate relations between France and Germany. But the French had never forgiven the driving of Delcassé out of office, and the result of the Algeciras conference had not healed the wound. Besides this, there was the undying question of Alsace-Lorraine.

The outcome of the precarious situation, says the ex-Chancellor, was that England, following her traditional policy of balancing the Powers of Europe, was taking a firm position on the side of France and Russia, while Germany was increasing her naval power and giving a very definite direction to her policy in the East.

The commercial rivalry between England and Germany was being rendered acute politically by the growth of the German fleet. In this state of things Bethmann Hollweg formed the opinion that there was only one thing that could be done, to aim at withdrawing from the Dual Alliance the backing of England for its anti-German policy. The Emperor entirely agreed with him, and it was resolved to attempt to attain this purpose by coming to an understanding with England.

Reading between the lines, it is pretty obvious that the ex-Chancellor was at times embarrassed by the public utterances of his imperial Master. Him he defends throughout the book with conspicuous loyalty, and is emphatic about his desire to keep the peace, a desire founded in religious conviction. But the Emperor's way was to see only one thing at the moment. I translate a passa[5]ge from his Chancellor's book:

> "If from time to time he indulged in passionate expressions about the strong position in the world of Germany, his desire was that the nation, whose development beyond all expectation was filling him with conscious pride, should be spurred on to a fresh heightening of its energies. He sought to give it a continuous impulse with the energy of his enthusiastic nature. He wished his people to be strong and powerful in capacity to arm for their defense, but the German mission, which was for him a consuming faith, was yet to be a mission of work and of peace. That this work and this peace should not be destroyed by the dangers that surrounded us, was his increasing anxiety. Again and again has the Kaiser told me that his journey to Tangier in 1904, as to which he was quite unaware that it would lead to dangerous complications, was undertaken much against his own will, and only under pressure from his political advisers. Moreover, his personal influence was strongly exerted for a settlement of the Morocco crisis of 1905. And the same sense of the need of peace gave rise to his attitude during the Boer War and also during the Russo-Japanese War. To a ruler who really wanted war, opportunities for military intervention in the affairs of the world were truly not lacking.

> "Critics in Germany had in that period frequently pressed the point that a too frequent insistence in public on our readiness for peace was less likely to further it than, on the contrary, to strengthen the Entente in its policy of altering the *status quo*. In a period of Imperialism in which the talk about material power was loud, and in which the preservation of the peace of the world was considered only accidentally, like the ten years before the war, considerations such as these are undoubtedly full of significance, and perhaps the same sort of thing explains a good deal of strong language on the part of the Kaiser about Germany's capacity in case of war. It is certain that such utterances did not lessen the feeling of nervousness that filled the international atmosphere.

---

[5] In both cases I am writing with the books before me in the original.

But the true ground of such nervousness was the policy of the balance of power, which had split Europe into two armed camps full of distrust of each other. The Ambassadors of the Great Powers knew the Kaiser intimately enough to realize what his intentions, in spite of everything, were, and it required an untruthfulness only explicable by the psychological effect of war to permit the suggestion of a hateful and distorted picture of him as a tyrant seeking for the domination of the world and for war and bloodshed."

I have translated this passage from the book because I think it is instructive in its disclosure of uneasy self-consciousness on the part of the author. Obviously, the Emperor made his quiet-loving Minister at times uncomfortable. I do not doubt that the Emperor really desired peace, just as Herr von Bethmann Hollweg tells us. Yet he not only indulged himself in warlike talk, but was surrounded by a group of military and naval advisers who were preaching openly that war was inevitable, and were instructing many of the prominent intellectual leaders in their doctrine. The Emperor may well have been in a difficult situation. But he was playing with fire when he made such speeches to the world as he frequently did. I believe him to have most genuinely desired to keep the peace. But I doubt whether he was willing to pay the price for entry on the only path along which it could have been made secure. He was a man of many sides, with a genius for speaking winged words as part of his equipment. He was a dangerous leader for Germany under conditions which had already caused even a Bismarck concern. The result was that the world took him to be the ally, not of Bethmann Hollweg, but of Tirpitz, and what that meant we shall see when we come to the latter's book. I can not say that I think the judgment of the world was other than, to put the matter at its lowest, the natural and probable result of his language, and I find nothing in the ex-Chancellor's volume to lead me to a different conclusion.

The argument of that volume is that England should never have entered the Entente, for that by doing so she strengthened France and Russia so as to enable them to indulge the will for war. He assumes that there was this will as beyond doubt. But suppose England had not entered the Entente, what then? On Herr von Bethmann Hollweg's own showing France and Russia would have remained too weak to entertain the hope of success in a conflict with the Triple Alliance. Germany could, under these circumstances, have herself compelled these Powers to an entente or even an alliance. England would have been in such a case left in isolation in days in which isolation had ceased to be "splendid." For great as was her navy, it could not have been relied upon as sufficient to protect her adequately against the combined navies of Germany, France, Russia, and Austria, with that of Italy possibly added. It was the apprehension occasioned by Germany's warlike policy that made it an unavoidable act of prudence to enter into the Entente. It was our only means of making our sea power secure and able to protect us against threats of invasions by great Continental armies. The Emperor and his Chancellor should therefore have thought of some other way of securing the peace than that of trying to detach us from the Entente.

The alternative was obvious. Germany should have offered to cease to pile up armaments, if our desire for friendly relations all round could be so extended as to bring all the Powers belonging to both groups into them, along with England. But the German policy of relying on superior strength in armaments as the true guarantee of peace did not admit of this. I am no admirer of the principle of the balance of power. I should like to say good-bye to it. I prefer the principle of a League of Nations, if that be practicable, or, at the very least, of an Entente comprising all the Powers. But if neither of these alternatives be possible there remains, for the people who desire to be secure, only the method of the balance of power. Now Germany drove us to this by her indisposition to change her traditional policy and to be content to rely on the settlement of specific differences for the good feeling that always tends to result. She had, it is true, the misfortune for so strong a nation to have been born a hundred years too late. She had got less in Africa than she might have had. We were ready to help her to a place in the sun there and elsewhere in the world, and to give up something for this end, if only we could secure peace and contentment on her part. But she would not have it so, and she chose to follow the principle of relying on the "Mailed Fist." Of this policy, when pursued recklessly, Bismarck well understood the danger. "Prestige politics," as he called them, he hated. In February, 1888, he laid down in a well-known speech what he held to be the true principle. "Every Great Power which seeks to exert pressure on the politics of other countries, and to direct affairs outside the sphere of interest which God has assigned to it, carries on politics of power, and not of interest; it works for prestige." But that principle was not consistently followed by William the Second. Into the detailed story of his departure from it I have not space to enter. But those who wish to follow this will do well to read the narrative contained in an admirable and open-minded book by Mr. Harbutt Dawson, "The German Empire from 1867 to 1914," in the second volume of which the story is told in detail.

Instead of trying to alter the traditional attitude of Germany to her neighbors, Herr von Bethmann Hollweg let it continue. That he did not want it to continue I am pretty sure. At page 130 of his book he appeals to me, personally, to recall the words he used in a conversation we had one evening in February, 1912, words in which he sought to show me that "a proper understanding between our two nations would guarantee the peace of the world, and would lead the Powers by degrees from the phantom of armed Imperialism to the opposite pole of peaceful work together in the world." I remember his words, and with them I would remind him that I wholly agreed. I had myself used similar language in anticipation, and had begged him not to insist on our accepting an obligation of absolute neutrality under all conditions which might prove inconsistent with our duty of loyalty to France, now a friendly neighbor, a duty which rested on no military obligation, but on kindly feeling and regard. It was such friendship and mutual regard that I was striving, with the assent of the British Cabinet, to bring about with Germany also, and by the same means through which it had been accomplished in the case of France. Not by any secret military convention, for we had entered into no communications which bound us to do more than study conceivable possibilities in a fashion which the German General Staff would look on as mere matter of routine for a country the shores of which lay so near to those of France, but by removing all material causes of friction. And when Herr von Bethmann Hollweg adds of my reply that "even he preferred the power of English Dreadnoughts and the friendship of France," I must remind him of the words sanctioned beforehand when submitted by me to Sir Edward Grey, with which I began our conversation. I reproduce them from the record I made immediately after the conversation to which I have already referred in the preceding chapter, on which I again draw for further minor details. And I wish to say, in passing, that both Herr von Bethmann Hollweg and Admiral von Tirpitz have given in their books accounts of what passed in my conversations with them which tally substantially, so far as the words used are concerned, with my own notes and recollections. It is mainly as to the inferences they now draw from my then attitude that I have any controversy with them, and, in the case of Admiral von Tirpitz, to some slight inaccuracies which have arisen from misconstruction.

The ex-Imperial Chancellor asked the question whether I was to talk to him officially, the difficulty being that he could not divest himself of his official position, and that it would be awkward to speak with me in a purely private capacity. I said I had come officially, so far as the approval of the King and the Cabinet was concerned, but merely to talk over the ground, and not to commit either himself or my own Government at this stage to definite propositions. At the first interview, which took place in the British Embassy, on Thursday, February 8, 1912, and lasted for more than an hour and a half, I began by giving him a message of good wishes for the Conversations and for the future of Anglo-German relations, with which the King had entrusted me at the audience I had before leaving London. I proceeded to ask whether he wished to make the first observations himself, or desired that I should begin. He wished me to begin, and I went on at once to speak to him in the sense arranged in the discussions I had with Sir Edward Grey before leaving London.

I told him that I felt there had been a great deal of drifting away between Germany and England, and that it was important to ask what was the cause. To ascertain this, events of recent history had to be taken into account. Germany had built up, and was building up, magnificent armaments, and, with the aid of the Triple Alliance, she had become the center of a tremendous group. The natural consequence was that other Powers had tended to approximate. I was not questioning for a moment Germany's right to her policy, but this was the natural and inevitable consequence in the interests of security. We used to have much the same situation with France, when she was very powerful on the seas, that we had with Germany now. While the fact to which I had referred created a difficulty, the difficulty was not insuperable; for two groups of Powers might be on very friendly relations if there was only an increasing sense of mutual understanding and confidence. The present seemed to me to be a favorable moment for a new departure. The Morocco question was now out of the way, and we had no agreements with France or Russia except those that were in writing and published to the world.

The Chancellor here interrupted me, and asked me whether this was really so. I said it was so, and that, in the situation which now existed, I saw no reason why it should not be possible for us to enter into a new and cordial friendship carrying the two old ones into it, perhaps to the profit of Russia and France, as well as of Germany herself. He replied that he had no reason to differ from this view.

He and I both referred to the war scare of the autumn of 1911, and he observed that we had made military preparations. I was aware that the German Military Attaché in London had reported at that time to Berlin that we had so reorganized our army as to be in a position, if we desired to do so, to send six of our new infantry divisions and at least one cavalry division swiftly to France. The Chancellor obviously had this in his mind, and I told him that the preparations made were only those required to bring the capacity of our small British Army, in point of mobilization for eventualities which must be clear to him, to something approaching the standard of that celerity in its operations which Moltke had long ago accomplished for Germany and which was with her now a matter of routine. For this purpose we had studied our deficiencies and modes of operation. This, however, concerned our own direct interests, and was a purely departmental matter concerning the War Office, and the Minister who had the most to do with it was the one who was now talking to him and who was not wanting in friendly feeling toward Germany. We could not run the risk of being caught unprepared.

As both Herr von Bethmann Hollweg and Admiral von Tirpitz have devoted a good deal of attention to these and other conversations in their books, I have felt at liberty here and in the last chapter to state what, I am bound to observe, had better not, as it seems to me personally, have been held back for so long—the exact nature of that which actually passed when I was sent to Berlin in February, 1912. Accordingly, it is only necessary that I should add here a few words more about what indeed appears in most of its detail from the versions given by the two German Ministers concerned themselves.

I refused, not only because I had been instructed to do so, but because in my own opinion it was vital that I should refuse, to negotiate excepting on the basis of absolute loyalty to the Entente with France and Russia. The German Government asked for a covenant of absolute neutrality. This I could not look at. I had the same feeling about such an agreement for unconditional neutrality as Caprivi had when he was asked to renew the Reinsurance Treaty which Bismarck made with Russia at Skiernevice in 1884, and under which, notwithstanding that Germany might come to owe a duty to Austria to support her as her military Ally, he bound Germany to observe neutrality in case Russia were attacked by her. So far as appeared this Reinsurance Treaty probably had suggested the wording of the analogous formula which the Chancellor was proposing to myself. But altho we were not under the obligation to France which Germany was under to Austria in 1884, I felt, to use the words of Caprivi himself, when he succeeded Bismarck, and was asked to renew the engagement with Russia, that the arrangement was "too complicated" for my comprehension. It would have been not only wrong to expose a friendly France to the risk of being dismembered by an unjustifiable invasion, while her friend England merely stood looking on, but it would also have been prejudicial to our safety. For to have allowed Germany to take possession of the northern ports of France would have been to imperil our island security. The Chancellor was entitled to make the request he did, but I was bound to refuse it. I also, at the same time, told him that if Germany went on increasing her Navy, any agreement with us meant to lead to better relations would be little more than "bones without flesh." Germany might, indeed, as he had said, need a third training squadron, in addition to the two she had already in the North Sea. This we could easily meet by moving more of our ships to northern waters, without having to increase the number we were building independently. But if she had the idea of adding to her fleet on a considerable scale we should be bound to lay down two keels to every one of her new ships, and the inevitable result would be, no proportionate increase in her strength relatively to ours, but of a certainty a good deal of bad feeling.

I may observe that at the date of this conversation the new German Fleet Bill had not been made public, and we knew nothing of its contents in London, excepting that a third squadron for training was to be added to the two which were already there. For this purpose it had been said that a few ships and a moderate increase in personnel would be all that was required. Before I left Berlin the Emperor, as I mentioned in the preceding chapter, handed to me, with friendly frankness and with permission to show it to my colleagues, an advance copy of the new Bill. It looked to me as if, when scrutinized, its proposals might prove more formidable than we had anticipated. But I asked his permission to abstain from trying to form any judgment on this question without the aid of the British Admiralty, and I put it in my pocket and handed it to the First Lord of the Admiralty at a Cabinet held on Monday, February 12, in the afternoon of the day on which I returned to London. I was not very sure as to what might prove to be contained in this Bill, and my misgivings were confirmed by our Admiralty experts, who found in it a program of destroyers, submarines, and personnel far in excess of anything indicated in the only rumors that had reached us. After we had to abandon the idea of getting Germany to accept the carefully guarded formula of neutrality which was all that we could entertain, the Cabinet sanctioned without delay the additions to our navy which were required to counter these increases. Our policy was to avoid conflagration by every effort possible, and at the same time to insure the house in case of failure.

I felt throughout these conversations that the Chancellor was sincerely desirous of meeting me in the effort to establish good relations between the two countries. But he was hampered by the difficulty of changing the existing policy of building up armaments which was imposed on him. In only one way could he manage this, and that was by getting me to agree to a formula of absolute neutrality under all circumstances. The other, the better, and the only way that was admissible for us, the way in which we had surmounted all difficulties with France and Russia, he was not free to enter on, tho I believe that he really wished to. Hence the attempt at a complete agreement failed. But, as he says himself, much good came of these initial conversations, and still more of the subsequent conversations which followed on them in London between Sir Edward Grey and the German Ambassador. Candor became the order of the day, minor difficulties were smoothed over, and a treaty for territorial rearrangements, of the general character discussed in Berlin, was finally agreed on, and was likely to have been signed had the war not intervened.

As to the rest of the narrative in the ex-Chancellor's book, this is not the place to deal with it. His view that Germany was doing her best to moderate the rash action in Vienna which resulted in the declaration of war on Serbia, while England was doing much less to restrain the course of events at St. Petersburg, is not one which it is easy to bring into harmony with the documents published. This is a part of the history of events before the war which has already been exhaustively dealt with by others, and it is no part of the purpose of these pages to write of matters about which I have no first-hand knowledge. For I had little opportunity of taking any direct part in our affairs with Germany after my final visit to that country, which was in 1912. My duties as Lord Chancellor were too engrossing.

There are, however, in this connection just two topics toward the end of the book which are of such interest that I will refer to them before passing away from it. The first is the story that there was a Crown Council at Potsdam on July 5, 1914, at which the Emperor determined on war. This Herr von Bethmann Hollweg denies. He explains that in the morning of that day the Austrian Ambassador lunched with the Emperor, presumably at Potsdam, and took the opportunity of handing to him a letter written by the Emperor of Austria personally, together with a memorandum on policy drawn up in Vienna. This memorandum contained a detailed plan for opposing Russian enterprise in the Balkan peninsula by energetic diplomatic pressure. Against a hostile Serbia and an unreliable Roumania resort was to be had to Bulgaria and Turkey, with a view to the establishment of a Balkan League, excluding Serbia, to be formed under the ægis of the Central Powers. The Serajevo murder was declared to have demonstrated the aggressive and irreconcilable character of Serbian policy. The Austrian Emperor's letter endorsed the views contained in the memorandum, and added that, if the agitation in Belgrade continued, the pacific views of the Powers were in danger. The German Emperor said that he must consult his Chancellor before answering, and sent for Bethmann Hollweg and the Under-Secretary, Zimmermann. He saw them in the afternoon in the park of the Neues Palais at Potsdam. The Chancellor thinks that no one else was present. It was agreed that the situation was very serious. The ex-Chancellor says that he had already learned the tenor of these Austrian documents, altho he did not see the text of the subsequent ultimatum to Serbia until July 22. It was determined that it was no part of the duty of Germany to give advice to her Ally as to how she should deal with the Serajevo murder. But every effort was to be made to prevent the controversy between Austria and Serbia from developing into an international conflict. It was useful to try to bring in Bulgaria, but Roumania had better be left out of account. These conclusions were in accordance with the Chancellor's own opinion, and when he returned to Berlin he communicated them to the Austrian Ambassador. Germany would do what she could to make Roumania friendly, and Austria was told that in any case she might rely on her Ally, Germany, to stand firmly by her side.

The next day the Emperor set off in his yacht for the northern seas. The Chancellor says he advised him to do this because the expedition was one which the Emperor had been in the habit of making every year at that season, and it would cause talk if this usual journey were to be abandoned.

The other point relates to the date on which the German Chancellor saw the text of the Austrian ultimatum to Serbia. He tells us that it was brought to him for the first time on the evening of July 22 by Herr von Jagow, the Foreign Secretary, who had just received it from the Austrian Ambassador. The Chancellor says that von Jagow thought the ultimatum too strongly worded, and wished for some delay. But when he told the Ambassador this the answer was that the document had already been dispatched, and it was published in the Vienna *Telegraph* the next morning.

The conclusion of the Chancellor is that the stories of the Crown Council at Potsdam on July 5, and of the co-operation of the German Government in preparing the ultimatum, are mere legends. The question of substance as regards the first may be left for interpretation by posterity. As to the controversy about the second, it would be interesting to know whether Herr von Tschirsky, the German Ambassador at Vienna, knew of the ultimatum before it assumed the form in which it reached Berlin on July 22. I shall have more to say about these incidents later on when I come to Admiral von Tirpitz's account of them.

My criticism of Herr von Bethmann Hollweg is in no case founded on any doubt at all as to his veracity. I formed, in the course of my dealings with him, a high opinion of his integrity. But in his reasoning he is apt to let circumstances escape his notice which are in a large degree material for forming a judgment. This does not seem to me to arise from any deliberate intention to be otherwise than candid. I am sure that he believes that he is telling the full truth at all times. But he became a convinced partizan, quite intelligibly. This fact, however creditable to his patriotism, seems to me not only to explain why he thought it right to continue in office and stand by his country as long as he could through the war, but also to detract somewhat from the weight that would otherwise attach to the opinions of an honorable and well-meaning man.

I pass to the examination of the concurrent policy against which he could not prevail, and the existence of which takes the edge off his reasoning. That policy is expounded fully and clearly by Admiral von Tirpitz, a German of the traditional Military School, a man of great ability, and one who rarely if ever allowed himself to be deflected from pursuing a concentrated purpose to the utmost of his power.

Of the general character of this purpose his colleague, Bethmann Hollweg, was conscious, as appears from passages in the book just discussed, of which I have selected one for translation.

"The fleet was the favorite child of Germany, for in it the onward-pressing energies of the nation seemed to be most vividly illustrated. The application of the most modern technical skill, and the organization that had been worked out with so much care, were admired, and rightly so. To the doubts of those versed in affairs whether we were pursuing our true path by building great battleships, there was opposed a fanatical public opinion which was not disciplined in the interest of those responsible for the direction of affairs. Reflections about the difficult international troubles to which our naval policy was giving rise were held in check by a robust agitation. In the navy itself the consciousness was by no means everywhere present that the navy must be only an instrument of policy and not its determining factor. The conduct of naval policy had for many years rested in the hands of a man who claimed to exercise *political* authority over his department, and who influenced unbrokenly the political opinion of wider circles. Where differences arose between the Admiralty and the civilian leadership, public opinion was almost without exception on the side of the Admiralty. Any attempt to take into consideration relative proportions in the strength of other nations was treated as being the outcome of a weak-minded apprehension of the foreigner."

When I was in Berlin in 1912, the last year in which, as I have already said, I visited Germany, there were those who thought that Bethmann Hollweg would shortly be superseded as Chancellor by his powerful rival, Admiral von Tirpitz. But in these days the peace party in that country was pretty strong, and the then Chancellor was regarded as a cautious and safe man. It was later on, in 1913, when the new Military Law, with £50,000,000 of fresh expenditure, was passed, that the situation became much more doubtful. But the hesitation that existed in Government circles in Berlin earlier was never shared by the author of the "*Erinnerungen*," to which I now pass. One has only to look at the portrait at the beginning of that volume to see what sort of a man the author is. A strong man certainly, a descendant of the class which clustered round the great Moltke, and gave much anxiety at times to Bismarck himself.

The Admiral possesses a "General Staff" mind of a high order. A mind of this type has never been given a chance of systematic development in the English Navy, where the distinction between strategy and tactics, on the one hand, and administration on the other, has never been so sharply laid down as it has been, following the great Moltke, in Germany. Even Moltke himself was not satisfied with what had been accomplished in Germany in this direction by the Army. He is said to have complained that the General Staff building, which was put in the Thiergarten, while the War Office was in Berlin itself, near the corner of the Wilhelmstrasse, was only one mile distant from the War Office, when it should have been two. For he held that the exactness of demarcation of function, which was only to be attained if strategy and tactics were studied continuously by a specially chosen body of experts, could not be made complete if the War Office could get too easily at the General Staff. But what he accomplished at least gave rise to a school of exact military thought far in advance of any that had preceded it. The fruits of this were reaped in the war with Austria in 1866, and still more in that with France in 1870. And when the navy was first organized this principle was introduced into its organization, first by Stosch and then by Caprivi. Both of these had been trained in the great Moltke's ideas, and it was because of this that, altho soldiers, they were chosen to model the organization of the German Navy. It is true that we have beaten the German Navy. That was because, as Tirpitz himself admits, we possessed, not only superior numbers, but a tradition of long standing and a spirit in our fleet which Germany had not built up. But we shall do well not to overlook what he has to say about the procedure of basing strategy and tactics on exact knowledge, and careful study, especially when such ideas as that of landing small expeditionary forces on enemy territory by means of a naval expedition, are being considered, nor what he says of his efforts to make this procedure real. Numbers are not always sufficient. They are not likely to be large for a long time to come, and the study of all possibilities and of modern conditions is therefore more important than ever. The British Army knows this. It is not so clear that the British Navy is equally informed about the necessity of bearing the principle in mind.

ADMIRAL ALFRED P. VON TIRPITZ
LORD HIGH ADMIRAL OF THE GERMAN IMPERIAL NAVY
FROM 1911 TO 1916.

Tirpitz never served in the army, but he was brought up under the influence of these great soldiers. His first experience was indeed mainly in technical matters of construction. But he never let go the true principle of an Admiral or War Staff, and the result was that he considered, and not wholly without reason, that he was leading the German Navy on lines which were in the end likely to make it, when fully developed, a more powerful instrument than the British Navy. Instead of studying merely the lessons of the past, as we here seek them in, for instance, the history of the Seven Years' War of more than a century and a half ago, or in the operations of Nelson carried out a hundred years since, he insisted that the German Navy should study systematically modern problems, and in particular combined naval and military operations. In England we had no War Staff for the Navy until 1911, and our Senior Admirals disliked the idea. Consequently such staff study of military problems has never been properly developed, the wishes of our junior naval officers notwithstanding. In Germany the idea was regarded as a vital one throughout by Tirpitz.

The first chapter of Tirpitz's book describes the beginnings of the German Navy. The second deals with the Stosch period. The third is devoted to the administration of Caprivi during the time when he was head of the Admiralty, and extends to the period when he became Chancellor. The fourth is devoted to construction. The fifth describes the disastrous breaking up of the Naval Administration into Boards, to which the author says the Emperor William II. allowed himself to be persuaded. The sixth chapter is directed to tactical developments, a subject in which Admiral Tirpitz himself did much. The seventh deals with naval plans. The eighth contains a very interesting description of how he was sent to find a naval base in Chinese waters, and how he selected and developed, with German thoroughness, Tsingtau (Kiaochow). The ninth chapter begins the story of the difficulties he experienced when refused sufficient money and freedom while he was Minister of Marine. The tenth gives a vividly written account of his visits to Bismarck. The next five chapters are devoted to the development of the German Navy and its relation to foreign policy. The sixteenth, seventeenth, and eighteenth chapters are concerned with the author's views of the reasons for the outbreak of the war of 1914, and its history. The nineteenth is a chapter devoted to the submarine war, and to a farewell apostrophe to a Germany lost by bad leading and vagueness in objectives. There is also a supplement, containing letters written by him from time to time during the war, and his observations on what ought to have been the consistent policy of Germany in construction of battleships and submarines.

The great thesis of the book is that the only way to preserve the peace was to make Europe fear German strength, and that this imported such battle-fleets as would attract allies to Germany for protection, and would thus in the end weaken the Entente. England was the real enemy, and England could not be dislodged from her powerful position in the world so long as she was allowed to continue in command of the ocean. For Bethmann Hollweg's alternative policy of a peaceful *rapprochement* with England he has no words but those of contempt. He, too, he says, had ideas as to how to keep the peace, but they were diametrically different from those of his colleague the Chancellor. On him he pours scorn for his attempts at departure from the policy of Frederick the Great and Bismarck.

Tirpitz had been deeply impressed by the writings of Admiral Mahan. He himself drew from them the lesson that in ultimate analysis world-power for Germany depended on the sea-power which she had not got, and he set himself to build it up. He endeavored to educate on this subject, not only the Reichstag, where he says he had much opposition, but the public. Under Prince Bülow this was less difficult than he subsequently found it. His account of how the Minister of Education and the University professors helped him, and of how he contrived to enlist the Press, is as interesting as it is significant. But his great difficulty was obviously with William the Second. The Emperor had done much for fleet construction, and was so interested in it that he meddled at every turn in technical and strategical matters alike. The Ministry of Marine was not allowed to carry out the Admiral's own plans and conceptions. And when Bethmann came on the scene the situation became, according to the former, even worse. He moans over the apparent limitlessness of the money and authority with which the English Admiralty was provided by Parliament and the nation. At last he carried with his colleagues and in the Reichstag the policy of Fleet Laws, under which the Reichstag passed measures which took construction, in part at least, from off the annual navy vote, and he got through the succession of Acts that laid down programs extending over several years. Richter and other distinguished public men fought Tirpitz over these, but, in part at least, he got his way, and secured the nearest approach to continuity that his ever-supervising Sovereign would permit to him.

What Tirpitz says he asked for above everything was a definite policy for war, and this he could not get the leave of Bethmann to lay down, nor could he get the volatile Emperor to stick to definite conceptions of it. For coast defense he had a supreme contempt. The great German Army would take care of this, so far as invasion was concerned, and an adequate battle-fleet would do the rest. It is noticeable that apparently he never even dreamed of trying to invade England with her fleet protection. It was in quite another way that he intended, if necessary, to harass this country. He wanted to threaten our commerce and to be able to break any blockade of Germany. German sea-power was to be made strong enough to attract allies by its ability to rally all free nations without any curatorship by the Anglo-Saxons.

This is what he says his war objectives were. He bitterly complains of the opposition to them and to himself which he met with from such papers as the *Frankfurter Zeitung*, and from the influence of certain of his colleagues. Constitutionalism he appears to have hated. The democracy of Germany was not suited to such leading as Lloyd George, during the war, gave to England, and Clemenceau to France. In Germany, he declares, a strong hand is always required, and a revolution is inevitable in case the hand is weak, and defeat follows. For Germany needed "the Prussian-German State." The tradition of Frederick the Great and Bismarck was its protecting spirit.

Can we wonder, if the narrative of this capable man is accurate, that Bethmann struggled for his rival policy of conciliation in the face of almost insuperable difficulties? Tirpitz had a strong party at his back, both in Prussia and elsewhere. What made it strong was largely that its members shared his view of England and of the situation. "They looked to us," he says, "it was the last chance of international freedom." I thought in 1912 that Bethmann might in the end win, for in the main at that time the Emperor was with him, and so were Ballin and many others of great influence. The Social Democrats, too, were gaining influence rapidly. But the presence of a powerful school of thought at the back of Tirpitz, a school which, had it succeeded, would have secured the place it desired by reducing to a precarious state the life of my own country, made me feel that, while we must do all we could to extend our friendships so as to convert and bring in Germany, the chances of success did not preponderate sufficiently to justify relaxation of either vigilance in preparation or resolution in policy. My feeling remained what I had tried to express in the address delivered at Oxford in August of 1911. "I wish," I said then, "all our politicians who concern themselves with Anglo-German relations, those who are pro-German as well as those who are not, could go to Berlin and learn something, not only of the language and intellectual history of Prussia, but of the standpoint of her people — and of the disadvantages as well as the advantages of an excessive lucidity of conception. Nowhere else in Germany that I know of is this to be studied so advantageously and so easily as in Berlin, the seat of Government, the headquarters of *Real-politik*, and it seems to me most apparent among the highly educated classes there."

Bismarck does not appear to have known much while in office about Tirpitz, and when the latter desired later on to enlist his outside support he did not find it at first easy. But, having with some difficulty got the assent of the Emperor to a new ship being named after Bismarck, he in the end got from the latter permission to visit him at Friedrichsruh in 1897. There Tirpitz arrived at noon. The family were at luncheon. He tells us how the Prince sat at the head of the table, and how he rose, cool but polite, and remained standing till Tirpitz was seated. The Prince assumed the air of one suffering from sharp neuralgic pain, and he kept pressing the side of his head with a small indiarubber hot-water bottle. It was only with an appearance of difficulty that he uttered, and his food was minced meat. However, when he had drunk a bottle and a half of German champagne (*Sect*) he became animated. After the dishes were removed, Countess Wilhelm Bismarck lit his great pipe for him, and with the other ladies quitted the room. The atmosphere was one of gloomy silence. But the great man suddenly broke it by raising his formidable eyebrows, and directing a grim look at Tirpitz, whom he appears next to have asked whether he himself was a tomcat that needed only to be stroked in order to procure sparks to be emitted. Tirpitz then timidly unfolded his plans and his policy of building big battleships. Bismarck was critical, and turned his criticism to other matters also. He denounced as disastrous the abrogation by Caprivi and William the Second of the treaty he (Bismarck) had made with Russia for Reinsurance. Bismarck declared that, in case of an Anglo-Russian war, our policy was contained in the simple words: neutrality as regards Russia. The modest Tirpitz ventured to suggest that only a fleet strong enough to be respected could make Germany worthy of an alliance in the eyes of Russia and other powers. Bismarck rejected this almost angrily. The English he thought little of. If they tried to invade Germany the Landwehr would knock them down with the butt-ends of their rifles. That a close blockade might knock Germany down never seemed to occur to him.

However, in the end Tirpitz says that the Prince became mollified and expressed agreement with the view that an increased fleet was necessary.

Bismarck then invited the Admiral to go with him for a drive in the forest. Despite the neuralgia, this drive, which took place amid showers of rain, lasted for two hours. The carriage, moreover, was open. There were two bottles of beer, one on the right and the other on the left of the Prince, which they drank on the way, and he smoked his pipe continuously. "It was not easy to keep pace with his giant constitution."

For the details of the conversation, which was conducted in English so that the coachman might not understand it, I must refer the reader to the chapter in which it is described. The old warrior spoke with affection of the Emperor Frederick, but as regarded his son William, he appears to have let himself go. Tirpitz was to tell the latter that he, Bismarck, only wanted to be let alone, and die in peace. His task was ended. He had "no future and no hopes."

Tirpitz saw Bismarck twice subsequently. The last time was on the occasion of a surprize visit to him by the Emperor. This visit was not wholly a success. The conversation got on to unfortunate lines. Bismarck began to speak of politics, and the Emperor ignored what he said and did not reply. The younger Moltke, who was present, whispered to Tirpitz, "It is terrible," alluding to the Emperor's want of reverence. When the Emperor left, his Minister, von Lucanus, who was with him, held out his hand to the old Prince. But Lucanus had formerly intrigued against him. Consequently he "sat like a statue, not a muscle moved. He gazed into the air, and before him Lucanus made gestures in vain."

All this notwithstanding, Tirpitz seems to have made a good impression. For after these visits the Bismarck press began to speak favorably of him.

But I must not linger over side issues. The book is so full of interesting material that in writing about it one has to resolve not to be led away from the vital points by its digressions. One of these points is that to which I have already made reference in giving the Chancellor's views about it, the responsibility for what happened in July, 1914, and in particular for the decision taken on the 5th of that month at Potsdam.

It is interesting to compare Tirpitz's account of the meeting that took place then, on the invitation of the Emperor, with that of Bethmann, altho the former was not present, and bases his judgment only on what was reported to him as Minister. He gives an account of what happened which makes the meeting seem a more important one than the ex-Chancellor takes it to have been. The Admiral's view is that at this date what was urgently wanted was "prompt and frank" action. Austria should not have been allowed to rush upon Serbia, however just her causes for anger. On the other hand the German Emperor should have at once and directly appealed to the Czar to co-operate with him in endeavoring to secure such a response to reason and expression of contrition on the part of Serbia as would have eased off the situation, which was full of danger. For, with an unfriendly Entente interesting itself, no war which broke out was likely to be capable of being kept localized.

Tirpitz was not in Berlin on July 5, but he received reports from there of what was happening. Neither he nor von Moltke, the Chief of the General Staff, was consulted, but Tirpitz declares that the Emperor saw at Potsdam the Minister of War, von Falkenhayn, and also the Minister of the Military Cabinet, von Lyncker. If so, whether or not the conference was technically a Crown Council, the meeting was a very important one.

Tirpitz confirms Bethmann in saying that, prompted by chivalrous feeling, the German Emperor responded to the Emperor of Austria by promising support and fidelity. He declares that the Emperor William did not consider the intervention of Russia to protect Serbia as probable, because he thought that the Czar would never support regicides, and that, besides, Russia was not prepared for war, either in a military or financial sense. Moreover, the Emperor somewhat optimistically presumed that France would hold Russia back on account of her own disadvantageous state of finance and her lack of heavy artillery. The Emperor did not refer to England; complications with that country were not thought of. The Emperor's view thus was that a further extension of dangerous complications was unlikely. His hope was that Serbia would give in, but he considered it desirable that Germany should be prepared in case of a different issue of the Austro-Serbian dispute. It was for that reason that he had on the 5th commanded the Chancellor, Bethmann Hollweg; the Minister of War, von Falkenhayn; the Under-Secretary of State for Foreign Affairs, Zimmermann; and the Minister of the War Cabinet, von Lyncker, to Potsdam. It was then decided that all steps should be avoided which would attract political attention or involve much expense. After this decision the Emperor, on the advice of the Chancellor, started on his journey to the North Cape, for which arrangements had already been made. The duty of the Chancellor under the circumstances was to consider any promise to be given to Austria from the standpoint of German interests, and to keep watch on the method of its fulfilment. The Chancellor, says his critic, did not hesitate to accept the decision of the Emperor, apparently imagining that Austria's position as a Great Power was already shaken and would collapse unless she could insist on being compensated at the expense of the greedy Serbians. He probably had in his mind the success obtained in the earlier Balkan crisis over Bosnia and Herzegovina. He goes on to tell us that he was not informed as to what the Emperor was thinking of during his tour in northern waters, but that he had reason to believe that he did not anticipate serious danger to the peace of the world. And he observes, as a characteristic of the Emperor, that when he was not apprehensive of danger he would express himself without restraint about the traditions of his illustrious predecessors, but the moment matters began to look critical his became a hesitating mood. The Admiral thinks that if the Emperor had not left Berlin, and if the full Government machinery had been at work, means might have been found by the Emperor and the Ministry of averting the danger of war. As, however, the Chief of the General Staff, the Head of the Admiralty Staff, and Tirpitz himself were kept away from Berlin during the following weeks, the matter was handled solely by the Chancellor, who, being in truth not sufficiently experienced in great European affairs, was not able to estimate the reliability of those who were advising him in the Foreign Office.

COUNT LEOPOLD BERCHTOLD
MINISTER OF FOREIGN AFFAIRS OF AUSTRIA-HUNGARY
FROM FEB. 1912 TO JAN. 1915.

Von Tirpitz goes on to say that by July 11 the Berlin Foreign Office had heard that the Entente had advised yielding at Belgrade. The Chancellor, he declares, could now have brought about a peaceful solution, but, convinced as he was that the Entente did not mean war, he drew the shortsighted conclusion that Austria, without considering the Entente, might force a march into Serbia and yet not endanger the world's peace. His optimism was disastrous. On July 13 he (the Chancellor) was, according to Tirpitz, informed of the essential points in the proposed Austrian ultimatum. Bethmann, as already stated, says that he did not see the ultimatum itself until the 22nd, when it had already been dispatched. But he does not say that he had been given no forecast of its contents from the German Ambassador at Vienna. Tirpitz quotes, but without giving its exact date, a memorandum sent to him at Tarasp apparently just after the 13th. It was forwarded from the Admiralty, and was in these terms: "Our Ambassador in Vienna, Herr von Tschirsky, has ascertained privately, as well as from Count Berchtold, that the ultimatum to be sent by Austria to Serbia will contain the following demands: I. A proclamation of King Peter to his people in which he will command them to abstain from greater Serbian agitation. II. Participation of a higher Austrian official in the investigation of the assassination. III. Dismissal and punishment of all officers and officials proved to be accomplices."

Tirpitz says that his first impression, when he received this document in Tarasp, was that Serbia could not possibly accept the terms of such an ultimatum. And he adds that he believed neither in the possibility of localizing the war nor in the neutrality of England. In his view the greatest care was required to reassure the Russian Government, especially as England would wish "to let war break out in order to establish the balance of power on the Continent as she understood it." But the Chancellor expressed the wish that he should not return to Berlin, for his doing so might give rise to remarks. If this be so, it seems to have been a very unfortunate step. The Emperor and his most important Ministers should all have been in Berlin at such a time. Bethmann's advice appears intelligible only if he thought, as is quite possible, that he could himself handle the negotiations best if the Emperor and Tirpitz were both out of the way. If so, he was not successful. He did not in the end respond to Sir Edward Grey's wish for a conference, and earlier he had failed to bridle the impulsive ally who was dashing wildly about. It looks as tho, however good his intentions may have been, he was taking terrible risks.

Now this was the crucial period. Grey was doing his very utmost to avert war, and was even pressing Serbia to accept the bulk of what was in the ultimatum. As to his real intentions, I may, without presumption, claim to be better informed than Admiral von Tirpitz. Sir Edward Grey and I had been intimate friends for over a quarter of a century before the period in which the Admiral, who, so far as I know, never saw him, diagnoses the state of his intentions. During the eight years previous to July, 1914, we had been closely associated and were working as colleagues in the Cabinets of Sir Henry Campbell-Bannerman and Mr. Asquith. And in that July, throughout the weeks in question, Sir Edward was staying with me in my house in London, and considering with me the telegrams and incidents, great or small.

It is a pure myth that he had, at the back of his mind, any such intentions as the Admiral imagines. He was working with every fiber put in action for the keeping of the peace. He was pressing for that in St. Petersburg, in Paris, in Berlin, in Vienna, and in Belgrade. He was not in the least influenced either by jealousy of Germany's growth or by fear of a naval engagement with her, as Tirpitz infers. All he wanted was to fulfil what, for him, was the sacred trust that had been committed to him, the duty of throwing the whole weight of England's influence on the side of peace. And that was not less the view of Mr. Asquith, whom I knew equally intimately, and it was the view of all my colleagues in the Cabinet.

Germany was going ahead with giant strides in commerce and industry, but we had not the slightest title to be jealous or to complain when she was only reaping the fruits of her own science and concentration on peaceful arts. I had said this myself emphatically to the Emperor at Berlin in 1906 in a conversation the record of which has already been given. There was no responsible person in this country who dreamt, either in 1914 or in the years before then, of interfering with Germany's Fleet development merely because it could protect her growing commerce. What responsible people did object to was the method of those who belonged to the Tirpitz school. The peace was to be preserved; I give that school full credit for this desire; but preserved on what terms? On the terms that the German was to be so strong by land and sea that he could swagger down the High Street of the world, making his will prevail at every turn.

But this was not the worst, so far as England was concerned. The school of von Tirpitz would not be content unless they could control England's sea power. They would have accepted a two-to-three keel standard because it would have been enough to enable them to secure allies and to break up the Entente. Now it was vital to us that Germany should not succeed in attaining this end. For if she did succeed in attaining it, not only our security from invasion, but our transport of food and raw materials, would be endangered. With a really friendly Germany or with a League of Nations the situation would have mattered much less. It was the policy of the school to which Tirpitz and the Emperor himself belonged which made the situation one of growing danger and the Entente a necessity, for these were days when other nations near us were beginning to organize great battle-fleets. If Bethmann Hollweg's policy had prevailed there would have been no necessity for any such Entente as was the only way of safety for us. But he could not carry his policy through, earnestly tho he desired to do so, and thus provide the true way to permanent peaceful relations. I think he believed that the only use Britain ever contemplated making of her Navy, should peace continue, was that of a policeman who co-operates with others in watching lest anyone should jostle his neighbor on the maritime highway. He believed in the *Sittlichkeit*, which we here mean when we speak of "good form." But that was not the faith of his critics in Berlin. They wanted to have Russia, and if possible France also, along with their navies, on the side of Germany. Peace, yes, but peace compelled by fear—a very unwholesome and unstable kind of peace, and deadly for the interests of an island nation. Hence the Entente!

What we had to do was to prevent, if we could, the Tirpitz school from getting its way, and we tried this not without some measure of success. Even to-day our pacifists now join with chauvinist critics of a policy which was pursued steadily for many years, and was that of Campbell-Bannerman as well as of Asquith. They reproach us for having entered on our path without having adequately increased our naval and military resources. The reproach is not a just one. It is founded on a complete misconception of the true military situation. It is only necessary to read carefully through Admiral von Tirpitz's very instructive volume to see that he took precisely the same view as we did, and as was held to unswervingly by our

Committee of Imperial Defense. England's might lay in final analysis in her sea power. She needed also a small but very perfect army, capable of high rapidity in concentration by the side of the great French Army, in order to prevent the coasts of France close to our own from being occupied by an enemy invading French territory.

In his book the Admiral refers to a letter I wrote to *The Times* on December 16, 1918, pointing this out and the grounds on which the strategical conception was based. The Admiral expresses his agreement, and says that it was a fatal blunder of the German Highest Command not to use their submarine power at the very outbreak of the war to prevent our Expeditionary Force from crossing the Channel and co-operating in resisting the German advance towards Calais. From there Germany could have commanded the Channel and bombarded London.

So he says, and we were quite aware all along that he might well think so. The other thing that he makes plain by implication is that the direct invasion of England was never contemplated by Germany in the face of our command of the sea. I had long ago satisfied myself that this was the German view, by a study of their military textbooks and from conversations with high German officers. But, what was more important than what I personally thought, the Committee of Imperial Defense, on which I sat regularly during eight years, was clear about it, and this after close study, and after hearing what the most eminent exponents in this country of a different view had to urge before them.

Consequently our military policy was not doubtful. No doubt it would have been a nice thing could we have possessed in 1914 a great army fashioned and trained, not for firing rifles on the seashore, but for a struggle on French and Belgian soil. But such an army would have taken two generations at least to raise and train in peace time, and if we had laid out our money on it after 1870 instead of on ships, we should not have had the sea power which Tirpitz says gave us "bulldog" strength. In strategy and in military organization you can not successfully bestride two horses at once. He who would accomplish anything has to limit himself. Possibly it was because this was not clearly kept in view even in Germany that the volume before us is an exposition of a thesis which is novel in these islands, that it was not England that was unprepared, but Germany herself. For the confusion of objectives that led to this Tirpitz blames Bethmann's peace policy, the parsimony of the Reichstag, and the Emperor's failure to attain to clear notions about war aims.

He criticizes me for saying that there was in Germany before 1914 a war party alongside of a peace party. It was really only the Bethmann group, he declares, that believed in peace being built on anything else than preponderance in armed power. The tradition of the German nation and the view of all sensible statesmen in Germany, *e.g.*, Prince Bülow and the Emperor himself as a rule, was that the foundation of a lasting peace could only be laid with armaments. Now if this is so it is plain how the war came about. The "shining armor" oration in Austria, some years before war broke out, was simply one among many illustrations which so alarmed civilized nations that they huddled together for protection against this school of statesmen. Bethmann's was the true policy had he been allowed to carry it out. It is possible that he thought he had a better chance of carrying it out than could have been the case were they to be present, when he got the Emperor and Tirpitz to keep away from Berlin after the meeting at Potsdam on July 5. Unfortunately he underestimated the tendencies of Berchtold, Conrad von Hoetzendorf, Forgasch, and others in Vienna, who, with no misgivings such as those of Tirpitz as to the outcome, had determined on *"losgehen."* The proximate cause of the war was Austrian policy. A secondary cause was the absence of any effective attempt at control from Berlin. The third and principal cause was the Tirpitz theory of how to keep the peace, the theory that had come down from Frederick the Great and his father, and was barely a safe one in the hands of even a Bismarck.

The only circumstances that could have justified Germany in her tacit encouragement to Austria to take a highly dangerous step—a step which was almost certain to bring Russia, France, and England into sharp conflict with the Central Powers—would have been clear proof that the three Entente nations were preparing to seize a chance and to encircle and attack Germany or Austria or both.

Now for this there is no foundation whatever. Russia, whatever Isvolsky and other Russian statesmen may have said in moments of irritation over the affair of Bosnia and Herzegovina, did not want to plunge into war; France did not desire anything of the kind; and, as for England, nothing was more remote from her wishes. It was only in order to preserve the general peace that we had entered the Entente, and the method of the Entente policy, the getting rid of all specific causes of difference, was one which had nothing objectionable in it. We urged Germany also to enter upon this path with us. We offered to help her in her progress toward the attainment of a "place in the sun." The negotiations which took place with Sir Edward Grey in London after my return from Berlin in 1912 are evidence of our sincerity in this, for they culminated in agreement on the terms of a detailed Treaty, under which a vast number of territorial questions were settled to mutual satisfaction. We did not either in 1912, as Admiral von Tirpitz appears to imagine, in the conversation at the Schloss, or later on, offer territory that was not our own but belonged to Portugal, or Belgium, or France. The contrary is evident from the fact that the British government pressed Germany to consent to the immediate publication of the draft Treaty, agreed early in 1914, when signed. All we did on both occasions was to propose exchanges with Germany of territory that was ours for territory that was hers, to undertake not to compete for the purchase of certain other territory that might come into the market, in consideration of a corresponding undertaking on her part, and to agree about zones within which each nation should distribute its industrial energies and give financial assistance to undertakings.

The gallant Admiral gives an account of the meeting which took place on February 9, 1912, in the Emperor's Cabinet room in the Schloss between himself, the Emperor and myself. He represents me as making a "generous offer of colonial territories which the English neither possessed nor of which they had the least right of disposal, in order to flatter the Kaiser's desires." Now in this impression the Admiral was wholly wrong. What I spoke of was what I have just referred to, exchanges of parts of our own territory for parts belonging to Germany, and undertakings such as I have just referred to. These things I had considered the previous day with the Chancellor, and I do not think the Emperor was in the least under the impression which von Tirpitz entertained. The matter was indeed not one with which the Department of the Minister of Marine was likely to be familiar. My suggestions were made in accordance with my instructions, and were, of course, *bona fide* in all respects. What I was pressing for was the means for making possible a slackening in naval construction on both sides, and for acceptance of the Entente and of our position in it. What I desired was to extend its friendly relations so as to bring Germany and Austria and Italy within them and get rid of anxiety about the balance of power and the growth of armaments. I think the Emperor throughout understood this, and certainly the Chancellor did. Tirpitz appears to have suspected, in an attitude in which I was only aiming at being friendly and even cordial, concealment of an encircling and aggressive purpose. After studying his book I do not wonder! When one rises from reading it one understands the fixity of an idea, which amounted to an obsession, and compelled him to believe in the necessity for what would have amounted to the overthrow of Britain as a Great Power.

From the Emperor, on this as on other occasions, I met with nothing but the kindliest of receptions. Admiral von Tirpitz describes the luncheon party which preceded the conference in the Cabinet Room. He speaks of a certain *"spanning"* or tension which prevailed during the luncheon which the Emperor and Empress gave to the Berlin Cabinet and myself, and of restraint in the conversation. I can not say that I perceived any of these things, but then, of course, I was a foreigner. What I do remember was the general kindly feeling and the evident satisfaction produced by the production of the famous red champagne and great cigars with which the Emperor regaled his guests. For myself, special distinction was reserved. For, before proceeding to business, the Emperor read to me Goethe's poem, *Ilmenau*, of which he thought I might like to be reminded before we sat down to our task. He then observed that, out of consideration for Tirpitz, we must confer in German, while on the other hand this would be the harder on me because the naval matters with which we had to deal were not in my department, as they were in that of the Admiral. This was, of course, true. And then, in compensation for disadvantages which, as he said, would otherwise be unfair, he smilingly remarked that he had a plan for adjusting the balance of power on this occasion. He insisted on my occupying the Imperial chair, which stood at the head of the narrow Cabinet table, while His Majesty himself should sit on an ordinary chair on my left hand and the Admiral on another on my right. I thought that these arrangements suggested the possibility of a tough controversy, and as far as the Admiral was concerned it proved to be so. For the discussion lasted for two and three-quarter hours, and was fairly close. I said throughout that, while I came here to explore the ground with the authority of my Sovereign and his Cabinet, I had come, not to make a treaty at that stage, but on a preliminary voyage of discovery with a view to taking back materials with which the Cabinet of St. James's might be able to construct one, and that I had been delighted with the graciousness of my reception. I mention this because the Admiral appears not to have quite understood my position. I have no doubt that the Emperor understood it.

At the end of the conversation I felt for once a little tired, and was glad when the Emperor asked von Tirpitz to drive me back to the Hotel Bristol. I thought the manner of the latter during the journey highly polite and correct, but not wholly sympathetic. I can only say that on my part I had endeavored to put every card I had upon the table.

COUNT OTTOKAR CZERNIN

MINISTER OF FOREIGN AFFAIRS OF AUSTRIA-HUNGARY
FROM DEC. 1916 TO APRIL, 1918.

I have now touched on what seem to me the salient points in both of the volumes by these two famous statesmen. I have, I hope, brought out sufficiently the fact that on their own showing they were pursuing contradictory policies, and that it was the consequent failure to follow a policy that was consistent and continuous that in the end led Germany to the slippery slope down which she glided into war. The circumstances of the world before and in 1914 were so difficult, the piling up of armaments had been so great, that nothing but the utmost caution could secure a safe path. I believe the Emperor and Bethmann to have desired wholeheartedly the preservation of the peace. But to that end they took inadequate means, and the result was a disastrous failure to accomplish it.

The disturbing presence of the policy of relying on a preponderance in power over England, to be gained by a great navy, to the side of which the smaller navies would be attracted, imposed on England the necessity of guarding against what was menacing the national life. As the outcome of this situation she was compelled, so long as Germany insisted on developing her naval policy, to sit down and take thought. The result of her deliberations may be summed up in eight propositions:

1. It was necessary, if the safety of England by sea was not to be put in jeopardy that she should enter into real and close friendships with other nations.

2. The great attraction to these other nations would lie in the maintenance of British sea power.

3. While the power of the British Navy was of the first importance to France, she might also, through no fault of her own, be placed in such peril as made it desirable that we should be able to render her help by land also.

4. But the military forces of France and her ally, Russia, were great enough to make it reasonable to estimate that a small army from England would be a sufficient addition to enable France to break the shock of an aggressive attack on her.

5. Even on purely military grounds it was impossible for Great Britain to raise in time of peace a great army for use on the Continent. The necessity of recruiting and educating the necessary corps of professional officers required to train and command such an army would have occupied at least two generations if the task were to be taken in hand in peace time. But it was possible to organize and prepare a small but highly trained Expeditionary Force, provided we discarded some of our old military traditions, and studied modern requirements and objectives in consultation with those who were best able to throw light on them.

6. Altho more than modern and scientific military organization on a comparatively small scale was not in our power, we could in carrying out even this much lay foundations which would enable expansion in time of war to take place.

7. In the result, as was believed here, and as Admiral von Tirpitz himself seems to have anticipated, sea power and capacity for blockade would decide the issue of the war. In this respect Germany seemed less well prepared than Great Britain.

8. The last thing wished for was war, and if we had to enter upon it we should do so only in defense of our own vital interests, as well as those of the other Entente Powers. Our entry, if it was to come, must be immediate and unhesitating. For if we delayed Germany might succeed in occupying the northern coast of France, and in impairing our security by sea.

I will conclude this chapter by appending an estimate of the Emperor William II, which is worth comparing with that of his German Ministers already referred to.

In the chapter on William II in Count Czernin's book on "The World War" there is a passage which may, I think, turn out to be pretty near the truth about the late Emperor's mood: "Altho the Emperor was always very powerful in speech and gesture, still, during the war he was much less independent in his actions than is usually assumed, and, in my opinion, this is one of the principal reasons that gave rise to a mistaken understanding of all the Emperor's administrative activities. Far more than the public imagine, he was a driven rather than a driving factor, and if the Entente to-day claims the right of being prosecutor and judge in one person in order to bring the Emperor to his trial, it is unjust and an error, as, both preceding and during the war, the Emperor William never played the part attributed to him by the Entente:

"The unfortunate man has gone through much, and more is, perhaps, in store for him.

"He has been carried too high, and can not escape a terrible fall. Fate seems to have chosen him to expiate a sin which, if it exists at all, is not so much his as that of his country and his times. The Byzantine atmosphere in Germany was the ruin of Emperor William; it enveloped him and clung to him like a creeper to a tree; a vast crowd of flatterers and fortune-seekers who deserted him in the hour of trial. The Emperor William was merely a particularly distinctive representative of his class. All modern monarchs suffer from the disease; but it was more highly developed in the Emperor William, and therefore more obvious than in others. Accustomed from his youth to the subtle poison of flattery, at the head of one of the greatest and mightiest States in the world, possessing almost unlimited power, he succumbed to the fatal lot that awaits men who feel the earth recede from under their feet, and who begin to believe in their Divine semblance.

"He is expiating a crime which was not of his making. He can take with him in his solitude the consolation that his only desire was for the best.

"It has already been mentioned that all the warlike speeches flung into the world by the Emperor were due to a mistaken understanding of their effect. I allow that the Emperor wished to create a sensation, even to terrify people, but he also wished to act on the principle of *si vis pacem, para bellum*, and by emphasizing the military power of Germany he endeavored to prevent the many envious enemies of his Empire from declaring war on him.

"It can not be denied that this attitude was often both unfortunate and mistaken, and that it contributed to the outbreak of war; but it is asserted that the Emperor was devoid of the *dolus* of making war, that he said and did things by which he unintentionally stirred up war.

"Had there been men in Germany ready to point out to the Emperor the injurious effects of his behavior and to make him feel the growing mistrust of him throughout the world, had there been not one or two but dozens of such men, it would assuredly have made an impression on the Emperor. It is equally true that of all the inhabitants of the earth the German is the one least capable of adapting himself to the mentality of other people, and, as a matter of fact, there were perhaps but few in the immediate entourage of the Emperor who recognized the growing anxiety of the world. Perhaps many of them who so continuously extolled the Emperor were really honestly of opinion that his behavior was quite correct. It is, nevertheless, impossible not to believe that among the many clever politicians of the last decade there were some who had a clear grasp of the situation, and the fact remains that in order to spare the Emperor and themselves they had not the courage to be harsh with him and tell him the truth to his face. These are not reproaches, but reminiscences which should not be superfluous at a time when the Emperor is to be made the scapegoat of the whole world."

CHAPTER IV

THE MILITARY PREPARATIONS

When more time has passed and heads have become cooler the critics will have to decide whether Great Britain was as fully prepared as she ought to have been for the possibility of the great struggle into which she had to enter in August, 1914. Hundreds of speeches have been made, and still more articles have been written, to demonstrate that she was caught wholly unready. On the other hand authoritative writers in Germany have made the counter-assertion that she had prepared copiously, not merely to defend herself, but to join in encircling and crushing Germany.

I shall venture to submit some reasons for saying that neither of these views is the true one. During the whole of the period between the commencement of 1906 and the autumn of 1914 I sat on the Committee of Imperial Defense and took an active part in its deliberations. For over six of these eight years I was Minister for War, and I was in continuous co-operation with the colleagues who were, like myself, engaged in carrying into execution the methods which we had gradually worked out. Such as the plans were, the preparations which they required were completed before the war. As to the bulk of these preparations I speak from direct knowledge.

The Expeditionary Force, the Territorial Force, and the Special Reserve had been organized under my own eye, by soldiers who had studied modern war upon what was in this country a wholly new principle. Before they took matters in hand not only was there no divisional organization, but hardly a brigade could have been sent to the Continent without being recast. For there used to be a peace organization that was different from the organization that was required for war, and to convert the former into the latter meant a delay that would have been deadly. Swift mobilization, like that of the Germans even in 1870, was in these older days impracticable.

All this had been changed for the Regular Army at home by the end of 1908, and it was after that year easy to mobilize. Other changes, also of a sweeping character, had been made to complete the new structure. On August 4, 1914, Lord Kitchener took delivery of an army in being, small, but not inferior in quality to the best that the enemy possessed. With the creation of the new armies, for which the Expeditionary Force was the pattern—and, indeed, with the general management of the war—I had very little to do. But I saw a good deal of Lord Kitchener, enough to impress me from the day when he became War Minister with his extraordinary individuality and his remarkable courage and energy, and to make me feel what an invaluable asset his personality was for putting heart into the British nation.

I have referred to my own and earlier part in the matter only to make plain that I do not speak about it from mere hearsay. And to say this has been necessary, because I shall have to submit some observations which, if true, do not harmonize with assertions made by some of the critics of the successive Governments which were at work on the business of preparation for possible contingencies between 1906 and 1914. I will, however, begin by making these critics a present of a definite admission. We never intended to create an army capable of invading or encircling Germany, and we should, in our own view, have found ourselves unable to do so even had we desired any such thing.

Our purpose was quite a different one. It was purely defensive. We knew how high a level of military organization had been attained in France. She had a large army, an army not so large as that of Germany, but comparable with it in quality. Her ally, Russia, also had a large army on the other side of Germany, altho one not so perfectly organized as that of France. By adding to the French military defensive forces a comparatively small British Expeditionary Force of very high quality, organized as far as possible on the principle about which von der Goltz, in the introduction to his famous book, "The Nation in Arms," had written, we could provide what that eminent writer had suggested would be formidable, could it be properly organized, even against the German masses of troops. In the introduction to his "Nation in Arms" he had declared that, "Looking forward into the future we seem to feel the coming of a time when the armed millions of the present will have played out their part. A new Alexander will arise who, with a small body of well-equipped and skilled warriors, will drive the impotent hordes before him, when, in their eagerness to multiply, they shall have overstepped all proper bounds, have lost internal cohesion, and, like the green-banner army of China, have become transformed into a numberless but effete host of Philistines."

This, of course, did not mean that the little Expeditionary Force could by itself cope with the admirably organized and enormous German Army, but it did point to the growing importance in these times of high morale and quality, and to the value that even a small force, if sufficiently long and closely trained, might prove to have, if placed in a proper position alongside the excellent soldiers of France. A careful study had made us think that the addition of even a small force of such quality to those of France and Russia would provide the combined armies with a good chance of defeating any German attempt at the invasion and dismemberment of France.

But in addition to and apart from all this, the British Navy had been raised before 1914 to a strength unexampled in its history, and Mr. Churchill had for the first time introduced in the autumn of 1911 the valuable principle of a war staff, fashioned with a view to the systematic study of modern naval war in co-operation with the forces on land.

These naval reforms had helped to confer the fresh power which took shape in the blockade which was in the end to prove decisive in the struggle. The heads of the newly organized Military General Staff met the representatives of the Admiralty War Staff at systematically held meetings of the Committee of Imperial Defense, under the presidency of the successive Prime Ministers—first of Sir Henry Campbell-Bannerman and then of Mr. Asquith. Not only were the Ministers at the head of the Admiralty and the War Office present to listen to what their experts had to say and to assist in arriving at conclusions on the questions discussed at these meetings, but other Ministers (including Lord Crewe, Sir Edward Grey, Lord Morley, Mr. Lloyd George, and Lord Harcourt) attended regularly. The function of this committee was to consider strategical difficulties with which the nation might conceivably find itself confronted, and to work out the solutions. It was a committee the members of which were selected and summoned by the Prime Minister, to whom it was advisory. He determined the subjects to be investigated. Secrecy was of course essential, excepting so far as the Cabinet was concerned. The presence of the non-military Ministers to whom I have referred was a proper guarantee that from the Cabinet there was no desire to withhold information. Possible operations on the Continent of our army occupied much of the time of the committee. About the propriety of the conversations which took place between members of the General Staffs of France and England questions have been raised. But these conversations were concerned with purely technical matters, and doubts as to their justification will hardly arise in the minds of people who are aware what modern war implies in the way of preliminary inquiries as to its conditions.

We were not engaging in any secret undertaking. We were merely providing what modern military requirements had rendered essential. Without study beforehand by a General Staff military operations in these days are bound to fail. If at any time we had, by any chance whatever, to operate in France it was essential that our generals should possess long in advance the knowledge that was requisite, and this could only be obtained with the assistance of the General Staff of France itself. We committed ourselves to no undertaking of any kind, and it was from the first put in writing that we could not do so. The conversations were just the natural and informal outcome of our close friendship with France.

The French had said that if it was to be regarded as even possible that we should come to their assistance in resisting an attack, which might, moreover, result if successful in great prejudice to our own security in the Channel, we should find this study vital. Our General Staff took the same view, and at the request of Sir Edward Grey, who had written to him, I saw Sir Henry Campbell-Bannerman at his house in London in January, 1906. He was a very cautious man, but he was also an old War Minister. He at once saw the point, and he gave me authority for directing the Staff at the War Office to take the necessary steps. He naturally laid down that the study proposed was to be carefully guarded, so far as any possible claim of commitment was concerned, that it was not to go beyond the limits of purely General Staff work, and further that it should not be talked about. The inquiry into conditions thus set on foot was conducted by the three successive generals who occupied the position of Director of Military Operations—the late General Grierson, General Ewart, and General Wilson. Each of these distinguished soldiers from time to time explained the progress made in working out conceivable plans for using the Expeditionary Force in France and in more distant regions, to the full Committee of Imperial Defense, and obtained its provisional approval.

I should like to say how much the Committee of Imperial Defense, which was originally a very valuable contribution made by Mr. Balfour, when Prime Minister, to the organization of our preparedness for war, owed to its secretaries. To such men as Admiral Sir Charles Ottley and, after his time, to Colonel Sir Maurice Hankey, the nation is under a great debt, and it was the least that could be done to include the latter in the thanks of Parliament to the sailors and soldiers to whom our actual success was due. It was he who, assisted by a brilliant staff on which the late Colonel Grant Duff was prominent, planned and prepared that remarkable War Book, which was completed in excellent time before the outbreak of hostilities, and which contained full instructions for every department of Government which could be called on to assist if war broke out. Not only the drafts of the necessary orders, but those of the necessary telegrams, were written out in advance under Sir Maurice Hankey's instructions. He and Sir Charles Ottley, themselves sailors, formed real links between the navy and the army, and did an enormous amount of work in co-ordinating war objectives.

Of the Navy I need say nothing, for its preparations are well understood. Nor need I say much of the details in the reorganization of the army. The general principle of this was to complete the Cardwell system by shaping the home battalions into six great divisions, and so providing them with transport, munitions, stores, and medical and other equipment, as to make them instantly ready for war. The characteristic of the old British Army, as it was up to 1907, was, as I have already observed, that it lived in peace formations only, in small and detached units which would have to be refashioned into quite different formations before they could be ready to be sent to fight.

This state of things involved much delay in mobilization. A careful inquiry made in 1906 disclosed that in order to put even 80,000 men on the Continent, a period which might be well over two months was the minimum required. Besides this great difficulty, the other items to which I have referred as required for the six divisions were not there in any shape even approaching sufficiency. The artillery too was deficient.

There is no more amusing myth than the one according to which the horse and field artillery were reduced. The batteries which could be made instantly effective for war were, in fact, raised from forty-two to eighty-one. The personnel of this artillery was increased by a third for mobilization. For the first time the horse and field artillery was given the modern organization which Cardwell had not been able to give it. The establishments had been merely peace establishments. There were ninety-nine batteries which could parade about on ceremonial occasions, but if war had broken out they would have had to be rolled up, and the personnel of fifty-seven of them taken to produce the mobilized forty-two which were all that could be put into the field. The difficulty was got over by the organization of eighteen of the ninety-nine into training brigades, and the additional men needed for the mobilization of eighty-one fighting batteries were thus obtained. No doubt some of the artillery officers did not like being set to training work, and complained that they were being reduced. But it was a reduction from unreal work of parade in order to double fighting efficiency. Not a man or a gun of the regular horse and field artillery was ever reduced in any shape or form, and not only were the effective batteries largely increased, but over 150 serviceable batteries were created and made part of the Second Line, or Territorial, Army. This was a force which could be used either for home defense or for expansion of an expeditionary force of Regulars. The Militia, which was not under obligation to serve abroad, was abolished, and its substance was converted into third regular battalions, organized for the purpose of training and providing drafts to meet the wastage of war in the first and second regular battalions of their regiments. Some of those third battalions are said to have trained and sent out as many as twelve thousand men apiece in the course of the war.

All these things were done under the direction of such young and modern soldiers as Sir Douglas Haig on the General Staff side, and as Sir John Cowans on the administrative side. Both of these officers were brought home from India for the purpose. Sir Herbert Miles, as Quartermaster-General, and Sir Stanley von Donop, as Master-General of the Ordnance also rendered much help. The newly organized General Staff thought the plans out under the direction, first of Sir Neville Lyttelton, and then of Sir William Nicholson, its successive chiefs. The latter and Sir Douglas Haig in addition worked out, in consultation with the representatives of the Dominions, the organization of their troops in units and with staffs and weapons corresponding as nearly as was practicable to our own. Systematic conferences between the British and Dominion War and other Ministers prepared the ground for this. Sir Wilfrid Laurier and General Botha and others of the Dominion Ministers came to London and co-operated.

It is sometimes said that all these things were very well, but that we should have at once raised a much larger army, as in the course of the war we ultimately had to do. The answer is that in a time of peace we could not possibly have raised a large army on the Continental scale. If we had tried to we should have made a miserable and possibly disastrous failure. The utmost we could do toward it was to provide the organization in which the comparatively small force which was all we could create might be expanded after a war broke out.

How this nucleus organization, on the basis of which the later expansions took place, was fashioned so as to afford a general pattern, anyone may see who chooses to expend a shilling on the purchase of the little volume called "Field Service Regulations, Part II." This piece of work took nearly three years to prepare. With the organization of which I have spoken, which was made in accordance with its principles, the whole of the task of recasting the British Army was performed by 1911.

What we had by that time attained was the power to send an army of, not 100,000 men, which was all that had originally been suggested, but of 160,000, to a place of concentration opposite the Belgian frontier, and to have it concentrated there within a time which was fifteen days in 1911, but was a little later reduced to twelve. No German army could mobilize and concentrate at such a distance more rapidly. So far as I know none of the necessary details were overlooked, and the timetables and arrangements for the concentration worked out, when the moment for their use came, without a hitch. What had been done was to take the old-fashioned British Army and to rid it of superfluous fat, to develop muscle in place of mere flesh, and to put the whole force into proper training. If the warrior looked slender he was at least as well prepared for the ring as science could make him.

It is said that this army ought to have been provided from the first with more heavy artillery. But the reason why its artillery, and that of the French armies also, were of a comparatively light pattern was not due to any notion of economy or to civilian interference. We had enough money, even in those difficult days, for every necessary purpose.

The real reason was that the General Staffs of both the French and the British Armies had advised that the campaign would probably be one in which swiftness in moving troops would prove the determining factor. Heavy artillery, and even any large number of the ponderous machine-guns of that period (the Lewis gun had not yet appeared), would have been a serious impediment to such mobility. What was anticipated was a series of great battles. "It was supposed by certain soldiers," says a well-informed military critic (Colonel A'Court Repington, at page 276 of his "Vestigia"), "that the war against Germany would be decided by the fighting of some seven great battles *en rase campagne*, where heavies would be a positive encumbrance."

So far the staffs proved to be right, for in the early period of the war mobility did count for a very great deal, and it was not until later that trench warfare became the dominant factor, a stage for which even the Germans themselves, as we now know, from the memoirs of Admiral Tirpitz and other books, were not adequately prepared in point of guns, or of shells and powder, either.

It is said that we in Great Britain ought, before entering on the Entente, to have provided an army, not of 160,000, but of 2,000,000 men. And it is remarked that this is what we had to do in the end. This suggestion does not, however, bear scrutiny. No doubt it would have been a great advantage if, in addition to our tremendous navy, we could have produced, at the outbreak of the war, 2,000,000 men, so trained as to be the equals in this respect of German troops, and properly fashioned into the great divisions that were necessary, with full equipment and auxiliary services. But to train the recruits, and to command such an army when fashioned, would have required a very great corps of professional officers of high military education, many times as large as we had actually raised. How were these to have been got?

I sometimes read speeches, made even by officers who have served with distinction at the head of their men in the field, which express regret that the British nation was so shortsighted as not to have provided such an army before the war. They point to the effort it made later on with such success during the war. But to raise armies under the stress of war, when the people submit cheerfully to compulsion, and when highly intelligent civilian men of business readily quit their occupations to be trained as rapidly as possible for the work of every kind of officer, is one thing. To do it in peace time is quite another. I doubt whether more was possible in this direction than, in the days prior to the war, to organize the Officers' Training Corps, which contained over twenty thousand partially prepared young men, and began at once to expand to yet larger dimensions from the day when war broke out. For the corps of matured officers, required to train recruits and to command them in war when organized in their units, would have had to consist of soldiers, themselves highly trained in military organization, who had devoted their lives to this work as a profession. It takes many years in peace time to train such officers. Because they must be professional, they can only be recruited under a voluntary system.

Now, before the war it was difficult enough to recruit even so many as the number we then had got, a number totally inadequate for any army larger than the small one we actually put into shape at home. Every source had been tried in my time by the able administrative generals who were working under me at the War Office. I say "administrative generals," for here comes in the source of the confusion which at times leads not a few—including some whose military training has been exclusively in the leading of troops and in strategy and tactics—to miss the point.

Under the modern military principle, which is the secret of rapidity and efficiency in mobilization, duties are carefully defined and divided. The General Staff does not administer, and is not trained in the business of administration. This kind of military business is entrusted to the administrative side of the army, the officers of which receive a different kind of training. The General Staff says what is necessary. The administrative side provides it as far as it can. And among the exclusive functions of the administrative side of the War Office is the recruiting of personnel by the Adjutant-General and the Military Secretary. It is true that the Director of Military Training, who supervises the training of the young officer when obtained, belongs to the General Staff. That is because his work is educational. With obtaining the young officer it is only accidentally that he is at all concerned.

When, therefore, even distinguished commanders in the field express regret at the want of foresight of the British nation in not having prepared a much larger army before 1914, I would respectfully ask them how they imagine it could have been done.

To raise a great corps of officers who have voluntarily selected the career of an officer as an exclusive and absorbing profession has been possible in Germany and in France. But it has only become possible there after generations of effort and under pressure of a long-standing tradition, extending from decade to decade, under which a nation, armed for the defense of its land frontiers, has expended its money and its spirit in creating such an officer caste.

Now, the British nation has put its money and its fighting spirit primarily into its Navy and its oversea forces. Why? Because, just as the Continental tradition had its genesis in the necessity for instant readiness to defend land frontiers, so our tradition has had its genesis in the vital necessity of always commanding the sea.

Possibly if, just after the war of 1870, we had endeavored to enter on a new tradition, and to develop a great army, we might have succeeded in doing so. With forty years' time devoted to the task and a very large expenditure we might conceivably have succeeded. But I think that had we done so we should have been very foolish. Our navy would inevitably have been diminished and deteriorated. You can not ride two horses at once, and no more can you possess in their integrity two great conflicting military traditions.

But what I am saying does not rest on my own conclusions alone. In the year 1912 the then Chief of the General Staff told me that he and the General Staff would like to investigate, as a purely military problem, the question whether we could or could not raise a great army. I thought this a reasonable inquiry and sanctioned and found money for it, only stipulating that they should consult with the Administrative Staffs when assembling the materials for the investigation. The outcome was embodied in a report made to me by Lord Nicholson, himself a soldier who had a strong desire for compulsory service and a large army. He reported, as the result of a prolonged and careful investigation, that, alike as regarded officers and as regarded buildings and equipment, the conclusion of the General Staff was that it would be in a high degree unwise to try, during a period of unrest on the Continent, to commence a new military system. It could not be built up excepting after much unavoidable delay. We might at once experience a falling off in voluntary recruiting, and so become seriously weaker before we had a chance of becoming stronger. And the temptation to a foreign General Staff to make an early end of what it might insist on interpreting as preparation for aggression on our part would be too strong to be risked. What we should get might prove to be a mob in place of an army. I quite agreed, and not the less because it was highly improbable that the country would have looked at anything of the sort.

What we actually could produce in the form of an army had to be estimated, not as if we were standing alone, but as being an adjunct to what was possessed by France and Russia. They had large armies and small navies. We had a large navy and a small army. When these were considered in conjunction, I do not think that the hope of some of our best military authorities, that an aggressive attempt by the Central Powers could be made abortive, was an over-sanguine one.

Much of what we did owe for the excellence of the Expeditionary Force, such as it was in point of size, and much of what we have since owed for the excellence of the great armies that we subsequently raised, was due to the unbroken work of the fine Administrative Staff, developed in those days, to which I have already referred. I often regret that when the nation gave its thanks through Parliament to the army, the splendid contribution made by those who prepared the administrative services was not adequately recognized. But this arose from the old British tradition under which fighting and administration were not distinguished as being quite separate and yet equally essential for fighting. The public had not got into its head the reality of the process of defining the two different functions with precision, and of confiding them to different sets of officers differently trained.

The principle was a novel one in the army itself, and why one set of officers should be trained at the Staff College and another at the London School of Economics was not a question the answer to which was quite familiar, even to all soldiers.

It is, I think, certain that for purely military reasons, even if, in view of political (including diplomatic) difficulties any party in the State had felt itself able to undertake the task of raising a great army under compulsory service, and to set itself to accomplish it, say, within the ten years before the war, the fulfilment of the undertaking could not have been accomplished, and failure in it would have made us much weaker than we were when the war broke out. The only course really open was to make use of the existing voluntary system, and bring its organization for war up to the modern requirements, of which they were in 1906 far short. It is true that the voluntary system could not give us a substantially larger army, or more than a better one in point of quality. The stream of voluntary recruits was limited. When the 156 battalions of the line which existed on paper in 1906 were in that year nominally reduced to 148, there was no real reduction, altho some money was saved which was required for some other essential military purposes. For the remaining battalions were short of their proper strength, and it took all the recruits set free by the so-called reductions to bring the 148—some of which were badly short of officers and men alike—to the proper establishment required for the six new divisions of the Expeditionary Force.

I remember well the then Adjutant-General, Sir Charles Douglas, one of the ablest men of business who ever filled that position in this country, informing me at that time that he could not raise a single further division to be added to the six at home.

But if the voluntary system had disadvantages, it also presented us with advantages. The professional and therefore voluntary nature of our army, which, because it was professional, was always ready for sending overseas on expeditions, was in reality made necessary by our position as the island center of a great and scattered Empire. We had increased that Empire enormously by the possession of a voluntarily serving army. Whether this vast increase of the Empire has been always defensible I am not discussing. What I am saying is that we owe the actual increases largely to this, that we were the only Power in the world that was ready to step in at short notice and occupy vacant territory. We always had a much larger Expeditionary Force available for this special purpose than Germany or any other country. That has been our tradition, as contrasted with the tradition of other nations who have been limited in this kind of capacity by the necessity of putting their military forces on a compulsory basis and keeping them at home for the protection of their land frontiers. Ours was the method in which we had been schooled by experience.

It is for such reasons as I have now submitted that I am wholly unable to assent to the suggestion that we did not look ahead, or considered within the years just before the war whether we were preparing to make the sort of contribution that our own interests and our friendships alike required. Sea power was for us then, as always before in our history, the dominant element in military policy. I have little doubt that we made mistakes over details. That is inherent in human and therefore finite effort. But I believe that we did in the main the best we could for the fulfilment of our only purpose, which was to preserve the peace of the world and avoid contributing to its disturbance, and also to prepare to defend ourselves and our friends against aggression. Talk to the public we could not, for it would have hindered and not helped us to do so. A "preventive war," which the Entente Powers would not have been so ready to meet as they became later on, might well have been the result. Rhetorical declarations on platforms would have been wholly out of place. But we could think, and to the best of such abilities as we and our expert advisers possessed, we did try to think.

A curious legend which had its origin in Berlin, in October, 1914, has obtained such currency that it is worth while to make an end of it. The legend is that the British Military Attaché at Brussels, the late General Barnardiston, had informed the Chief of the Belgian General Staff of secret plans, prepared at the War Office in London, to invade Belgium, and if necessary to violate her neutrality, in order to make an expedition, the purpose of which was to attack Germany through that country. The story appears to have emanated from Baron Greindl, who was the Belgian Minister at Berlin in 1911. He had been completely misinformed, no doubt in that capital, and there is no truth whatever in what he had been told about what he called the "perfidious and naïf revelations" of the British Military Attaché at Brussels. Him the story represents as having said that his Minister (by whom I presume myself, as the then Secretary of State for War, to have been intended) and the British General Staff were the only persons in the secret. I have to observe, in the first place, that I never during my tenure of office, either suggested any such plan, or heard of anyone else suggesting it. When the story was brought to my knowledge, which was not until November, 1914, I inquired at once of General Barnardiston and of his successor, Colonel Bridges, whether there was any foundation for it. The reply from each of these distinguished officers was that there was none.

We were among the guarantors of Belgian neutrality, and it was of course conceivable that, if she called on us to do so, we might have had to defend her. It would be part of the duty of our Military Attaché to remember this, and, if opportunity offered, to ascertain in informal conversation the view of the Belgian General Staff as to what form of help they would be likely to ask us for. This he doubtless did, and indeed it appears from what the Chief of the Belgian General Staff wrote to the Belgian War Minister that the former had discussed the contingency of Belgium desiring our help with General Barnardiston, and had done so gladly. But even so the conversation must have been very informal, for in the account of it by the Chief of the Belgian General Staff there are errors about the composition of the possible British Force which indicate that either he took no notes, or else that Colonel Barnardiston had not thought it an occasion which required him to obtain details from London. At all events, such talk as there was appears to have had relation only to what we ought to do, if requested by Belgium to help, in case of her being invaded by another Power.

The documents will be found in the volume of Collected Diplomatic Documents relating to the outbreak of the war, presented to Parliament in May, 1915 (Cd. 7860). This volume includes a vigorous denial by Sir Edward Grey of the insinuation.

CHAPTER V

EPILOG

The great war is over, and the Powers of the West have conquered. In the earlier pages I have given my own view of why they won in the tremendous struggle that now belongs to history. They had on their side moral forces which were lacking to their adversaries.

Germany went into the war with a conviction that had been carefully instilled into her people. It was that she was being ringed round with the intention that she should be crushed, and that presently it would be too late for her to deliver herself. The lesson so taught to her was not a true one. She might easily have obtained guarantees of peace which ought to have satisfied her, without undertaking a risk which in the end was to prove disastrous. No one here wanted to ruin her, no one who counted seriously in this country. And if we did not want to, no more in reality did France or Russia. She brought her fate on her head by the unwisdom of her methods. But her people hardly desired the dangers of unnecessary war, and her rulers dared not have ventured these dangers had they not first of all preached a wrong doctrine to those over whom they ruled. They had their way in the end, and disaster to sixty-eight millions of Germans was the consequence. The calculations of their chiefs were bad from the beginning. It is almost certain that the best and most eminent among even these really desired peace. They blundered in method. It was not by continually flashing the saber that peace was to be secured.

It is scarcely likely that the conditions under which this war became possible will recur. It is more than unlikely that they will recur in our time. But it is none the less worth while to consider how the unlikelihood can be made to approach most nearly to a certainty.

Not, I think, by causing the millions of German-speaking people to feel that they are in chains without possibility of freedom. More certainly, surely, by leading them to the faith that if they will play a part in the great world effort for permanent peace and for reconstruction they will be welcomed to the brotherhood of nations. The individual German citizen is more like the individual Anglo-Saxon than he is different from him. The same hopes and the same fears animate him, and he is sober and industrious quite as much as we are. He has similar problems and similar interests.

Time must pass before the angry feeling that a great struggle produces can die down. But there are already indications that this feeling is not as intense with us as it was even a short time ago. Germany made a colossal and unjustifiable blunder.

She is responsible for the action of her late Government. We think so, and we are not likely to change our opinion on this point. The grief of our people over their dead, over the lives that were laid down for the nation from the highest kind of inspiration, will keep the public mind fixed on this conclusion. And so will the waste and misery to the whole world which an unnecessary war has brought in its train. But presently we shall ask ourselves, in moments of reflection, whether this ought to be our final word, and also, perhaps, whether some want of care on our own part, and certain deficiencies of which we are now more conscious than we used to be, may not have had something to do with the failure of other people to divine our real mood and intentions. I am not sure that in days that are to come we shall give ourselves the whole benefit of the doubt. However this may be, we are in no case a vindictive people.

But in any view something serious is at stake. It will be a bad thing for us, and it will be a bad thing for the world, if the people of the vanquished nations are left to feel that they have no hope of being restored to decent conditions of existence. At present despair is threatening them. Their estimate is that the crushing burden of the terms of peace, if carried out to their full possibilities, bars them from the prospect of a better future. Their only way of deliverance may well come to seem to them to lie in the grouping of the discontented nationalities, and the faith that by this means, at some time which may come hereafter, a new balance of power may begin to be set up.

Now this is not a good prospect, and the sooner we succeed in softening the sense of real hardship out of which it arises the better. Germany and Austria must pay the penalty they have incurred before the tribunal of international justice. But that penalty ought to be tempered by something that depends on even more than mercy. It is intended to be inflicted for the good of the world, and if it assumes a form which threatens the future safety of the world it is not wise to press it to its extreme consequences. We have to work toward a better state of things than that which is promised to-day. We have never hitherto kept up old animosities unduly long, and that has been one of the secrets of our strength in the world. The lessons of history point to the expediency of trying to heal instead of to keep open the wound which exists. Those who know the growth in the past of literature, of music, of science, of philosophy, of industry and of commerce, do not wish the German people to die out. It is only the ignorant that can desire this, and, hitherto in the course of our history, the ignorant have neither proved to be safe guides nor have they prevailed. To-day, as before, we must think of generations other than our own if we would preserve our strength.

I hope that a time is near in which we shall no longer proclaim old grievances, but instead cease to dwell on the past in this case, just as we have ceased in the cases of the French, the Spanish, the Russians, and the Boers. It is best in every way that it should come to be so.

It is not with any hope that these pages will satisfy the extremists of to-day that they have been written. They are intended for those who try to be dispassionate, and for them only, as a contribution to a vast heap of material that is being gathered together for consideration. It is well that those who were in any way directly connected with the story to which they relate should place on record what they saw. But the whole story in its fulness is beyond the knowledge of anyone of our time. The history of the world is, as has been said, the judgment of the world. It is therefore only after an interval that it can be sufficiently written. The ultimate and real origin of this war, the greatest humanity has ever had to endure, was a set of colossal suspicions of each other by the nations concerned. I do not mean that none of them were in the right or that some of them were not deeply in the wrong. What I do mean is that if there had been insight sufficient all round the nations concerned would not have misinterpreted each other.

To us it looks as tho Germany had been inspired throughout by a bad tradition, a spirit older than even the days of Frederick the Great. Had she been wise we think that she would have changed her national policy after Bismarck had brought it to unexampled success in things material. There are not wanting indications that he himself had the sense of the necessity of great caution in pursuing this policy farther, and felt that it could not be safely continued without modification. It was no policy that was safe for any but the strongest and sanest of minds, and even for those it had ceased to be safe. The potential resistance to it was becoming too serious.

But we do not need to doubt that there were many in Germany itself who saw this and did not desire to rely merely on blood and iron. The men and women in every country resemble those in other countries more than they differ from them. Germany was no exception to the rule. It is a great mistake to judge her as she was merely from a few newspapers and by the reports from Berlin of their special correspondents. Sixty-eight millions of people could not be estimated in their opinions by the attitude of a handful, however eminent and prominent, in the home of "*Real politik.*" It is, of course, true that the Germans were taught to believe that they were a very great nation which had not got its full share of the good things of this world, a share of which they were more worthy and for which they were better organized than any other. But it is also true that we here thought that we ourselves were entitled to a great deal to which other people did not admit our moral title. It was not only Germany that was lacking in imagination. No doubt many Germans had the idea that we wished to hem them in and that we did not like them. Our failure to make ourselves understood left them not without reason for this belief. But dislike of Germany was not the attitude of the great mass of sober and God-fearing Englishmen, and I do not believe that the counter-attitude was that of the bulk of sober and God-fearing Germans. They and we alike mutually misjudged each other from what was written in newspapers and said in speeches by people who were not responsible exponents of opinion, and neither nation took sufficient trouble to make clear that what was thus written and said was not sufficient material on which to judge it. It is very difficult to diagnose general opinion in a foreign nation, and one of the reasons of the difficulty is that people at home do not pay sufficient attention to the fact that their unfriendly utterances about their neighbors are likely to receive more publicity and attention than the utterances that are friendly. It makes little difference that the latter may greatly preponderate in number. They are read in the main only in the country in which they are made.

Neither Germans nor Englishmen were careful before the war always to be pleasant to each other, and the same used to be true of Frenchmen and Englishmen. But just as we are coming to understand why and how France and England misinterpreted each other systematically a century and a half ago, so we may yet learn how we came to present, more than a hundred years later, difficulties to the Germans not wholly unlike those which they presented to us. No mere record of the dry facts will be enough to render this intelligible in its full significance. The historian who is to carry conviction must do more than present photographs. He must create a picture inspired by his own study and from the depth of his own mind, and presented in its real proportions with its proper lights and shadows, as a true artist alone can present it. Browning has told us something worth remembering. It is at the end of "The Ring and the Book":

> Art may tell a truth
> Obliquely, do the thing shall breed the thought,
> Nor wrong the thought, missing the mediate word.
> So may you paint your picture, twice show truth,
> Beyond mere imagery on the wall, —
> So, note by note, bring music from your mind,
> Deeper than ever e'en Beethoven dived, —
> So write a book shall mean beyond the facts,
> Suffice the eye and save the soul beside.

The truth in its fulness and completeness can not be compassed in any single narrative of events. It is, of course, the case that history depends for its value on scientific accuracy, but that is not the only kind of truth on which it depends. No man, even the most careful and exacting, can rely on having the whole of the materials before his eye, and if he had them there they would not only be presented in tints depending on his outlook, but would be too vast to admit of his using more than isolated fragments to work into his picture of the whole. Selection is a necessity, and when to the fact that there must be selection there is added the other fact that every historian has his personal equation, the notion of a history constructed by a single man on the methods of the physicist is a delusion. The best that the great historian can do is to present the details in the light of the spirit of the period of which he is writing, and in order that he may present his narrative aright, as his mind has reconstructed it, he must estimate his details in the order in importance that was actually theirs. Now for this the balance and the measuring rod do not suffice. Quality counts as much as does quantity in determining importance. What is merely inert and mechanical is the subject neither of the artist nor the historian. It is, of course, necessary that by close and exact research the materials should first of all be collected and assembled. But that is only the first step, and it always has to be followed by a process of grouping and fashioning. The result may have to be the leaving out (or the leaving over for presentation by other artists) of aspects which are not dealt with. We see this when we compare even the best portraits. They do not wholly agree; it is enough if they correspond. For portraits may vary in expression, and yet each may be true. The characteristic of what is alive and is intelligent and spiritual is that it may have many expressions, every one of which really harmonizes with every other. It is because they can bring out expression in this fashion that we continue to set high store on the work of a Gibbon or a Mommsen.

The moral of this is twofold. We must, to begin with, be content for the present to remain in the stage at which all that can be done is to collect and assemble facts and personal impressions with as great care as we can. The whole truth we can not bring out or estimate until the later period, altho we may be sure enough of what we have before us to make us feel capable of doing justice of a rough kind, so far as necessary action is concerned.

And there is yet another deduction to be drawn. It is at all events possible that the wider view of a generation later than this may be one in which Germany will be judged more gently than the Allies can judge her to-day. We do not now look on the French Revolution as our forefathers looked on it. We see, because recent historians have impressed it on us, that it was a violent uprising against, not Louis XVI., but a Louis XIV. What France really made her great Revolution to bring about was the establishment of a Constitution. Horrible deeds were perpetrated in the name of Liberty, but it was not due to any horrible national spirit that they were perpetrated. France was responsible no doubt for the deeds of the men who acted in her name. But she could hardly have controlled them even had she passionately desired to do so. And she did not passionately desire to do so because, however little the mass of the people outside Paris may have wished to massacre the adherents of the old regime, the people as a whole welcomed deliverance from calamity, even at the price of violent action.

We judge the French nation wholly differently to-day from the way we judged it then, and it judges us differently. Yet it would have been well had we not in the end of the eighteenth century taken an exaggerated view of the French state of mind. We now realize that even so great a man as Burke mistook a fragment for the whole. Much blood and treasure might have been spared, and Napoleon might never have come into existence, had we and others been less hasty.

It is therefore a good thing to keep before us that it is at least possible that the verdict of mankind will be hereafter that when the victory was theirs the Allies judged the people of Germany in a hurry and reflected this judgment in the spirit in which certain of the terms of peace were declared. The war had its proximate origin in the Near East. It arose out of a supposed menace to Teuton by Slav. The Slavs were not easy people to deal with, and the Teutons were not easy people either. It was easy to drift into war. It may well prove true that no one really desired this, and that it was miscalculation about the likelihood of securing peace by a determined attitude that led to disaster. It is certain that the German Government was deeply responsible for the consequences. In the face of its traditional policy and of utterances that came from Berlin the members of that Government can not plead a mere blunder. None the less, a great deal may have been due to sheer ineptitude in estimating human nature. How much this was so, or how much an immoral tradition had its natural results, we can not as yet fully tell, for we have not the whole of the records before us. No one disputes that we were bound to impose heavy terms on the Central Powers. The Allies have won the war and they were entitled to reparation. This the Germans do not appear to controvert. They are a people with whom logic is held in high esteem. But we have to do something more than define the mere consequences of victory. We have also to make plain on what footing we shall be willing to live with the German nation in days that lie ahead. And here some enlargement of the spirit seems to be desirable in our own interests. We do not want to fall again into the mistake that Burke made.

The spirit is at least as important as the letter in the doctrine of a League of Nations. Such a League has for its main purpose the supersession of the old principle of balancing the Powers. In the absence of a League of Nations, or—what is the same thing in a less organized form—of an entente or concert of Powers so general that none are left shut out from it, the principle of balancing may have to be relied on. I believe this to have been unavoidable when the Entente between France, Russia and Great Britain was found to be required for safety if the tendency to dominate of the Triple Alliance was to be held in check. But in that case, and probably in every other case, reliance on the principle could only be admissible for self-protection and never for the mere exhibition of the power of the sword. If the principle is resorted to with the latter object the group that is suspected of aggressive intentions will by degrees find itself confronted with another group of nations that have huddled together for self-protection and may become very strong just because they have a moral justification for their action. It was this that happened before the war which broke out in 1914, and it was the state of tension which ensued that led up to that war. Had there been no counter-grouping to that of the Central Powers there would probably have been war all the same, but with this difference, that defeat and not victory would have been the lot of the Entente Powers.

Now the German-speaking peoples in the world amount to an enormous number, at least to a hundred millions if those outside Germany and Austria, and in the New World, as well as the Old, are taken into account. It may be difficult for them to organize themselves for war, but it will be less difficult for them to develop a common spirit which may penetrate all over the world. It is just this development that statesmen ought to watch carefully, for, given an interval long enough, it is impossible to predict what influence these hundred millions of people may not acquire and come to exercise. We do not want to have a prolonged period of growing anxiety and unrest, such as obtained in our relations with the French, notwithstanding the peace established by the Treaty of Vienna. Of the anxiety and unrest which were ours for more than one generation, the history of the Channel fortifications, of the Volunteer force and of several other great and often costly institutions, bears witness. Let us therefore take thought while there is time to do so. We do not wish to see repeated anything analogous to our former experience. The one thing that can avert it is the spirit in which a League of Nations has been brought to birth. That spirit alone can preclude the gradual nascence of desire to call into existence a new balance of power. It is not enough to tell Germany and Austria that if they behave well they will be admitted to the League of Nations. What really matters is the feeling and manner in which the invitation is given, and an obvious sincerity in the desire that they should work with us as equals in a common endeavor to make the best of a world which contains us both. One is quite conscious of the difficulties that must attend the attempt to approach the question in the frame of mind that is requisite. We may have to discipline ourselves considerably. But the people of this country are capable of reflection, and so are the people of the American Continent. The problem to be solved is one that presses on our great Allies in the United States, where the German-speaking population is very large, quite as much as it does on us. France and Belgium have more to forgive, and France has a hard past from which to avert her eyes. But she is a country of great intelligence, and it is for the sake of everybody, and not merely in the interest of our recent enemies, that enlargement of the spirit is requisite.

How the present situation is to be softened, how the people of the Central Powers are to be brought to feel that they are not to remain divided from us by an impassable gulf, this is not the occasion to suggest. It is enough to repeat that the question is not one simply of the letter of a treaty but is one of the spirit in which it is made. Conditions change in this world with a rapidity that is often startling. The fashion of the day passes before we know that what is novel and was unexpected has come upon us. The foundations of a peace that is to be enduring must therefore be sought in what is highest and most abiding in human nature.

INDEX

U

V

Lector House believes that a society develops through a two-fold approach of continuous learning and adaptation, which is derived from the study of classic literary works spread across the historic timeline of literature records. Therefore, we aim at reviving, repairing and redeveloping all those inaccessible or damaged but historically as well as culturally important literature across subjects so that the future generations may have an opportunity to study and learn from past works to embark upon a journey of creating a better future.

This book is a result of an effort made by Lector House towards making a contribution to the preservation and repair of original ancient works which might hold historical significance to the approach of continuous learning across subjects.

HAPPY READING & LEARNING!

LECTOR HOUSE LLP
E-MAIL: lectorpublishing@gmail.com

www.ingramcontent.com/pod-product-compliance
Lightning Source LLC
Chambersburg PA
CBHW020743160726
47993CB00006B/2585